THE REAL WITCHES'
HANDBOOK

THE

REAL WITCHES'
HANDBOOK

A Complete Introduction to the Craft

for Both Young and Old

KATE WEST

LLEWELLYN

Published in 2008 by Llewellyn Publications

First published by Thorson's,
an imprint of HarperCollins*Publishers* in 2001

Cover design by Kathryn Milton
Llewellyn is a registered trademark of Llewellyn Worldwide, Ltd.

Library of Congress Cataloging-in-Publication
Data available upon request.

ISBN-13 978-0-7387-1375-5

Llewellyn Publications
A Division of Llewellyn Worldwide, Ltd.
2143 Wooddale Drive, Dept. 978-0-7387-1375-5
Woodbury, Minnesota 55125-2989, U.S.A.
www.llewellyn.com

Printed in China

CONTENTS

ACKNOWLEDGEMENTS

No book is written without the help and assistance, patience and tolerance of a large number of people around the author. I would like to express my thanks to everyone who has helped, supported and encouraged me, most especially:

To everyone at HarperCollins, Mandrake Press and Pagan Media Ltd, who have encouraged me to write.

To Andy, Brian, Debbie, Keith, Lizzie, Lou and Steve, my proofreaders, whose expertise in a number of areas has proved invaluable.

Above all to my husband, Steve, and our son, Taliesin, for settling for a somewhat distracted wife and mother.

And to Julie for taking care of Taliesin, for feeding, cleaning encouraging, amusing and comforting him, leaving me free to sit at the keyboard.

Last but not least, to everyone of the Craft for the lessons they have taught me, whether deliberately or inadvertently!

INTRODUCTION

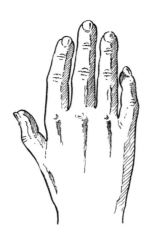

Welcome to The Real Witches' Handbook. This book is written for all those who are young to the Craft of the Witch, whether in years or in experience. Within these pages you can discover how Witchcraft can be practised by anyone who wishes to, even in this, our modern, crowded world. Welcome to a new way of thinking where you can take charge of your life and your destiny.

Today there is a new growth in spirituality and Witchcraft is one of the fastest-growing religions in the world. People are turning away from the better known patriarchal belief systems, with their rules and regulations. They are turning away from religions where they need an intermediary or priest to intercede and interpret their Gods for them. They are tired of being told what to believe, how to worship and what decisions they should make in their personal lives. They want to take charge of their lives, their morality and their beliefs. Having seen the mess that authority of one sort or another has made, people are no longer content to take on trust the information which is passed down to them. They want to talk to their God and/ or Goddess directly, and to worship in a way which seems natural and right to them.

Thanks largely to the World Wide Web and the Internet there is an increasing amount of information available on religions both old and new and an increasing openness about Witchcraft, which was previously a very reticent religion. As a result more and more people, of all ages and occupations and of both sexes, are becoming interested in Witchcraft, or 'the Craft', as it is also known. This interest is also being encouraged by fictional portrayals in books, films and TV. However, these come complete with many misconceptions and elaborations and it can be difficult for those new to the Craft to determine what is accurate and what is myth, especially if they have no one to guide them.

For the young it is especially hard as Witches have traditionally held that reputable Covens (the name for a group of Witches) do not accept members who are under 18 years old. This is partly because it is felt that the individual should have the opportunity to make an informed decision about their choice of spirituality (and therefore needs time to assess the options), partly because they should also have some life experience and maturity (although 18 is quite an arbitrary age to choose for this) and partly because taking on candidates under that age would (in most parts of the world) leave the group open to all kinds of accusations of corrupting minors.

This combination of increased interest and information leads to the modern Witch's dilemma: how to treat those who are under the age of 18? A few reputable groups have always had a policy of encouraging exceptional candidates, usually by a process of one-to-one support given by a senior member of the Coven, until such time as the 'age limit' has been passed. This support sometimes takes the form of supplying a formidable reading list and counselling patience, something which simply tends to alienate all but the most dedicated seeker. This is especially true as most of the better books were written a long time ago and were intended to be read by those who already had access to a group setting. In this day and age we have to recognize that from the age of 14, people are making decisions which could affect the rest of their lives, in exam choices for example, and at 16 they may set up home and/or marry.

There are also many mature people who live in the company of those who may not be tolerant of the study and practice of Witchcraft, and who may not be able to find, or travel to, a Coven which accepts newcomers.

The new enthusiast may set about discovering the Craft via the many books and websites that are available and quite often may end up setting off in the wrong direction, misled by some of the more dubious texts which abound. Additionally, and unfortunately, there have always been disreputable individuals and groups who are prepared to take advantage of earnest seekers, whether sexually or financially, and any Witch who turns away a prospective candidate is always aware that this is a lamentable possibility.

What I have set out to do with this book is to bridge these gaps and to dispel many of the misconceptions. Being a Witch, I believe that everyone is entitled to their own spirituality and that they are entitled to make an informed choice. Hence I feel there is a need to provide that information and in a way which is practical and usable under all but the most trying of domestic circumstances. This book is for all those who wish to explore this path whilst being sensitive to the needs of those around them.

Witchcraft has been described as 'a thinking person's religion' and this is a serious book about the Craft. It is written for all those who are serious about studying and practising, whether on their own or in preparation for joining a

Coven. Some of the content may seem a little dry to those who are keen to get on with the actual practice of Magic, but persevere, for all the parts are relevant to the understanding of the religion, ritual and Magic of Witchcraft. Think of the first couple of chapters as an introduction before the practical work of the rest of the book.

Use this as a workbook and make notes to record your own thoughts and feelings about what you are reading and in relation to the work you do in the Craft. In this way it will become not just a book to read, but also the foundation for your own Book of Shadows, the volume which forms the basis of every Witch's practice.

So for all the 'young in Craft' who would take charge of their future, for those inexperienced in spiritual variety, for those whose search for their own path has been exploratory, I offer an introduction to practising the oft misunderstood and misconstrued belief system of the Witch.

Blessed Be
Kate

ONE

WITCHCRAFT: THE MYTHS

Witches are normal everyday people, the kind you pass on the street without giving them a second glance or thought. They are men and women from all age groups, who have all kinds of jobs and normal family lives. They are just like everyone else; in fact they could be just anyone else. But you wouldn't think that if you were to look at the myths that have grown up about them.

The word 'Witch' conjures up many images. A Witch was a woman (for it usually was a woman) who lived on the edge of the village and who would heal the sick if treated well, but curdle your milk and spoil your crops if you upset her – or even curse your cattle, or your children, so that they would sicken and die. In return for her immortal soul she would have made a pact with the Devil for unnatural powers. And the Devil himself would accompany her in the form of a familiar, who in turn would feed off her flesh. Such Witches were supposed to gather together, flying by broomstick, so that they could join in orgies and meet the Devil in person.

A Witch might also be the old hag living alone in a tumbledown cottage in the forest, feared by all. In fairy tales, she would lure innocent children inside to eat them and drink their blood. Or the Witch might be a wicked fairy, not invited to the feast, who would curse the family as a result.

More recently the Witch's image has been influenced by books, music, films and TV. From *Bell, Book and Candle* to *The Craft*, *Bewitched* to *The X-Files* and *Buffy the Vampire Slayer*, Witches are now frequently portrayed as younger, attractive women. They are shown as having control over others. Using ancient powers they perform strange rituals (with lots of modern special effects) and conjure up spirits who do their bidding. They are seen to make people fall in love, to gain revenge on their enemies and even to conjure up uncompleted homework! In books they are often linked with Satanists, whose extensive powers enable them to live in improbably wonderful houses. And somehow along the way, Witches have been linked to the imagery of Goth and other forms of music, with their vampiric fashions, archaic black clothing, heavy make-up and jewellery.

Other things linked to Witchcraft include broomsticks, cauldrons and black cats, hooked noses, warts, pointed hats and billowing cloaks (black of course). The Full Moon and Halloween are thought to be especially 'Witchy' times.

Now, within these stories and images there are elements of truth, but they are hidden by exaggerations, fabrications and even political intrigue. To understand how these images arose, it is necessary to know a little about the background and history of the Craft.

Before Christianity became established (anything from 1,600 to 800 years ago in the various parts of Europe), there were other belief systems. Often called nature religions, these were based around the phases of the Moon, the cycles of the seasons, the land and the animals which lived on it. Different groups held different beliefs and worshipped different Gods and Goddesses, without conflict as far as we know. Roman Gods and Goddesses had shrines or temples alongside those of the native population. At first Christianity was just another belief system and its churches also co-existed peacefully. However, as it became linked with the Crown and the Government it became more powerful and in order to maintain control it sought to eradicate those earlier beliefs.

The Gods of the nature religions now came to be called devils or demons and their followers were accused of laying curses and practising foul Magic which ruined crops, sickened cattle and caused children to fall ill or to die. They were even accused of child murder and sacrifice. Stories were invented or altered to discourage people, especially children, from seeking to learn more. Special agents were appointed to hunt out the 'evil doers'. Special laws were introduced to cover their 'crimes'. Incentives, in terms of the land and money of those convicted, were provided to encourage people to report those neighbours and fellow villagers who might be involved in such 'demonic' activities.

There is nothing unusual in this – it is a process that has been, and still continues to be, repeated whenever the people of one faith seek to take control over the land, property and power of those of another. In the same way that after the Reformation one part of the Church sought to outlaw and eradicate another, so the Arabs and Jews are still fighting over Israel to this day.

But to return to the takeover of the nature religions, as a result of the Church's actions many innocent people were arrested, many were tortured and many were executed, some lawfully, others by the mob. Those who did wish to continue to follow the old religions did so secretly. They handed down their knowledge and beliefs by word of mouth and held their celebrations away from prying eyes. From the outside it appeared that Witchcraft had become a thing of the past, so much so that by the 1950s, it was no longer seen as a threat in Britain. The final remnants of the Witchcraft Act, first instituted in 1542, were finally repealed and Witches started, cautiously, to become more open once again.

The last 50 years have seen a great improvement in the way that people think about Witches and the Craft and media coverage is more favourable. Today, as a known Witch, I am less likely to have my windows broken or my tyres slashed than even 10 years ago, but there are still many misconceptions and I would like to address some of them here:

Witches are in league with the Devil and the same as Satanists.

Witches do not believe in, let alone worship, a devil. They do not believe in an evil being whose purpose is to balance out the good God. <u>Witches believe in personal responsibility</u> – we are each responsible for whatever we do, whether good or bad, and can blame no outside force (or devil) for those actions which we subsequently regret.

Nor is the practice of divination anything to do with conjuring up spirits who can see into the future. Divination is a way of accessing our own skills to see what is coming in our own and other people's lives.

Witches practise Black Magic.

Magic itself is neither good nor bad, white nor black, it is a neutral force in the same way as electricity is. If Magic is used in a positive and beneficial way it is often called 'white'; when used negatively it is often referred to as 'black'. However, most Witches try to adhere to the main 'rule' of the Craft, the Wiccan Rede, which states: 'An' it harm none, do what thou will.' Whilst there are undoubtedly a few Witches who do work Magic for selfish reasons or to the detriment of others, the vast majority of Magical workings are for the benefit of others.

Witches sacrifice animals.

Witches have a great respect for nature and for the rights of others. They do not believe that people have rights over animals or each other and do not make blood sacrifices. What they do sacrifice is time and energy. They may also make offerings of wine, oils, gemstones or items they have created themselves.

Witchcraft is all about sex and nudity.

Witchcraft is one of the ancient fertility religions. However, it is common to confuse fertility and sex. Fertility is not just about having babies, it is about inspiration, having new ideas. A fertile relationship is one where both partners assist one another to develop their individual potential to the full, where growth is encouraged, not restricted. This may or may not include having a family. A fertile business is one with new products, markets and customers.

It is also common to mistake the term 'nature religion' for 'naturist'. Naturists are those who prefer to remove their clothes as much of the time as possible, as they find this totally acceptable and a more comfortable way of being. There is nothing in the Craft which demands nudity, indeed one of the key tenets is that no one should ever be forced to do anything they are uncomfortable with. Some Witches do indeed work their rituals naked, or 'skyclad' as it is termed, while others work in robes or in special but everyday clothing. This is because changing what you wear marks the step between daily life and ritual working. Some Witches may also be naturists, but this tends to be more likely in the warmer parts of the globe!

Witchcraft is a 'pick and mix' religion.

Certainly the Craft overall has no set rituals or formulae and no defining text. As a Witch you can refer to the God or Goddess by different names at different times and you are expected to make your own judgements as to what is right and wrong on a day-to-day basis. There are no 'authorities' to tell you what to do, say and think.

There are many who feel that this all means Witchcraft cannot be a true religion – in other words, there are not enough rules! However, the Wiccan Rede, 'An' it harm none, do what thou will', whilst being a positive statement, is nevertheless a lot to live up to.

There is no proof that Witchcraft has any historical basis prior to the last 50 years.

It is true that there is little recorded history prior to the 1950s. Given the background of the persecution of Witches, not to mention the fact that writing was a skill available only to the privileged, this is hardly

surprising. However, a few documents have survived in private hands and there are of course the Church's own records, which seem to point to the continuation of the Craft. After all, why bother to persecute something which you do not believe exists? The absence of a long written 'pedigree' does not invalidate a belief system. Whether today's Witchcraft has been handed down as an intact religion, whether it is a renewed version of an older belief system or whether it has almost totally reinvented itself does not actually matter. What does matter is whether it is valid today for those who would practise it.

Witches have a hooked nose and warts.

As I once said in an interview, 'Well, I wouldn't be much of a Witch if I couldn't get rid of those!' Spreading the idea that Witches are ugly is simply another way of discouraging people from becoming interested in something that is not understood.

Witches are glamorous.

This is a more modern misconception. What you have to remember is that the people who make fictional TV programmes and films are rarely doing so in order to portray facts, they are in the business to attract an audience and make money – obvious when you think of it. However, there are still lots of people who believe, without thinking, that Witches all look like Buffy and Sabrina, etc., and that it is the Witchcraft which makes them look good. This is only accurate in that practising the Craft will make you feel better about yourself and encourage you to have respect for your mind, body and spirit. Additionally, because for most of us the imperfections we perceive are false or exaggerated, the self-honesty that the Craft requires will result in a more positive self-image.

Witches wear black.

Witches wear whatever they wish. They are not instantly recognizable by their clothes or the way they look. However, when working in groups, especially outdoors at night, Witches will often wear dark or black clothing, for two very practical reasons. First, if you are disturbed in your workings it is far easier for you to disappear if you blend into your surroundings. Witchcraft is not a spectator activity and no one wants to gather an audience of dog walkers or people returning from the pub who fancy a bit of light entertainment. Secondly, dark colours show the dirt less. Witches may be tending a fire or sitting on the ground or simply brush up against a tree – and light clothing generates extra laundry!

Witches wear a long cloak and pointed hat.

Many Witches do have a long cloak for use outdoors, as it covers clothing and keeps the weather out. It is especially useful if you wear robes. Also, a long dark cloak with a hood enables you to pull up the hood, step into the trees and become invisible to anyone but the most keen observer. The pointed hat, however, is not something many Witches will own unless they have a taste for fancy-dress parties. It is said by some to represent the cone of power which is often raised when working Magic. But as the cone of power is something on the psychic, rather than visible, plane it is hard to see how this became popularized as a pointy black hat, with or without symbols on it.

Witches wear lots of heavy make-up and jewellery.

Some do, many don't. The modern image of the Witch dressed in black, with long black hair, pale skin and darkened eyes, hung about with chains of silver, is partly generated by movies and TV, and partly by a fashion trend which some people are enjoying at present. Make-up and jewellery are fashion accessories or personal statements about the way you feel and the group you feel comfortable with, not requirements for Witchcraft.

A Witch lives with a black cat, a toad or other kind of familiar.

The belief that Witches have a familiar goes back to the time when it was usually the old and lonely who were accused of Witchcraft and these poor unfortunates often had a pet to keep them company. Many modern Witches do have a pet or pets – being a part of a nature religion inclines a person to seek the company of animals – but many do not keep pets. Toads, however, have never been all that popular!

Witches fly on broomsticks.

Witches fly on aeroplanes. The idea of flying to meetings on a broom is derived from the use of 'flying ointments'. These often poisonous ointments used to be made to heighten the senses, much in the way that some people today use drugs in a 'recreational' manner. The effect of some of the ingredients was to give the illusion of flight. Most Witches discourage the use of artificial aids to increase awareness, partly because such use can be dangerous (sometimes causing long-term physical and mental problems and occasionally death) and partly because if awareness or heightened senses are acquired or enhanced with drugs or herbs, they are not truly your own. It is, if you like, a second-rate form of enhancement compared to that which can be achieved through study and practice, and the use of artificial aids often slows down the development of unaided skills.

Witches do, however, use the broomstick, or 'besom' as it is also called, to sweep, whether practically as in removing autumn leaves from the garden or metaphorically in preparing a working space. The besom is also used in some kinds of fertility rituals to represent the union of male and female. At a Witch's wedding, or Handfasting, the couple will jump over the broom to symbolize the leap from their old lives into their new one and to encourage fertility – physical, mental and spiritual – in their union.

Witches brew strange concoctions in Cauldrons.

Witches who practise herbal work or who make ointments, salves and lotions tend to do so in the kitchen, in clean surroundings and comfort. These brews are often no stranger than any other natural remedy – indeed, they could be as normal as onion soup for a cold sufferer.

The Witches' Cauldron is often used to contain fire when working outside, or candles when working inside. This confines the flames so there is no risk of a fire getting out of hand and so that no damage is done to the surroundings. Sometimes a Cauldron is used to hold water as a symbol of the Goddess, or as an aid to divination or scrying (more on these later).

You may by now have noticed a number of main themes running through all these misconceptions:

* ✯ Everything nasty and frightening has been, or is, attributed to Witches and Witchcraft. People have a tendency to group together the same age-old fears whenever they are trying to put down the beliefs of others, especially when their own beliefs can become linked to the control of the people.

✴ Quite a few, but not all, of these accusations are built around a grain of truth. This is because it is easier to discredit someone if you build your propaganda around something they cannot deny. It is far harder to undo the damage, especially when it has had over 1,000 years to become part of people's beliefs.

✴ When it comes to appearance you cannot tell a Witch by the way they look – Witches are as individual as anyone else.

But by far the most insidious myth about the Craft is that Witchcraft makes life easier. Witchcraft does *not* make life easier. As a Witch, you will not have fewer problems, you will probably have more. Witchcraft is about hard work, study and self-discipline. It is about knowing when to speak or act and when to hold back.

If you practise Witchcraft you will almost certainly have to be careful about whom you tell about it and about what you tell, so you will have to learn to be very discreet. There will always be things which you need to keep secret, for example the names of those you have helped and their problems. As a Witch you must keep your word – you cannot give away the secrets of others, even though you may feel that this might solve a problem.

The Craft will give you the means to understand the way others think, feel and behave, and this understanding will eventually enable you to see that there are always two or more sides to every situation and many possible outcomes to every action. In time this knowledge will make you a better Witch, but often in the short term you will feel as though every potential action is going to fail. This can be the very time when you learn to wait and see.

For anyone who thinks that the Craft will make their life easier I would recommend that they give serious thought to the Wiccan Rede and the Rule of Three, both of which are explained in more detail in the next chapter.

TWO

WITCHCRAFT IN REALITY

Having looked at the misconceptions people have about Witches and Witchcraft, let us look at what Witches do believe in and practise.

One of the best definitions I have heard for a Witch is 'healer, teacher and parent'. The Craft has its roots in a time when people lived in small communities, when communication and travel, over even small distances, were the exception rather than the rule. The village Witch was the nurse, doctor, midwife, vet and counsellor for the community. Witches were the ones who held the knowledge of healing and prepared the medicines of their time. They were the ones whose study of human actions and human nature enabled them to help their friends, family and neighbours solve their problems and resolve their differences. They were the ones whose observation of nature enabled them to advise on when to plant crops and when to harvest, and how best to treat and keep the animals which provided food for the months ahead. They cared for the people, the land, the growth and the future of their community. As keepers of knowledge they also took the responsibility of selecting and training the next generation of healers and teachers.

Today's Witches often use the term 'near and dear' to refer to their community and, in a world where travel and communication are so much easier, this can extend to friends and Witches from far away. But the feeling is still that of family, whether through blood, fellowship in the Craft or simple friendship. The work is still that of healing, sharing knowledge and of caring for those in the immediate circle.

There are many kinds of Witch and many ways of practising the Craft and I shall talk about some of the better known variations later, but there are many common threads which link us together. To be strictly honest I should say that most Witches believe the following statements, but that their beliefs may be stated or emphasized in individual ways.

THE GODDESS AND THE GOD

Witches believe that the divine is both male and female, equally and in balance, and that we should strive for that balance both in ourselves and in our lives. Speaking practically, we believe that there is a Goddess as well as a God and that both are equally powerful, although some festivals and workings may be more appropriately directed to one or the other.

Both the Goddess and the God may be referred to by different names at different times, but this does not mean that each Witch believes that there are many Goddesses and many Gods. To illustrate this, think of a ball with many facets, similar to the kind seen at some concerts or discos. If each face of the ball is a different face of the Goddess or the God, there is still one ball, just as there is one Goddess and one God. If you were, say, working Magic with the aim of increasing your ability to study, you might wish to choose a different image, or facet, of the Goddess than you would if you were hoping to bring relief from illness for a friend.

Seeking the balance of male and female within us does not mean that we are seeking to become bi-sexual, rather that we respect and acknowledge the so-called male and female elements within our make-up. It is commonly thought that being assertive, logical and in control are masculine traits, whilst being sensitive, emotional and expressive are feminine ones. But we each have all these attributes to a greater or lesser degree and not accepting this, or being unable to use these skills, can make us very unhappy. Also, there are other, older stereotypes linked to gender: light, the Sun, daytime and good are seen as male; darkness, the Moon, the night and bad as female. Bringing these opposites into balance and seeing them for what they really are can enable us to see ourselves for what we are and what we are able to achieve. This personal balance is not simple to achieve, but is a task which accompanies us throughout life.

RESPECT FOR NATURE

We believe that we should respect nature and not take more than we need from the world around us. This does not mean that we worship nature, rather that we should care for our world and the things which grow and live upon it. We should also respect the natural order of things.

This takes many forms:

✺ Being economical with resources – not using the car when it isn't necessary, for example, and offering a lift to friends when we're all going the same way.

✵ Being aware of how much damage is done to the environment in order to satisfy our desires – for example, many crystals are mined from the Earth by strip mining and the use of explosives, devastating acres of land and the habitats of wildlife and people in order to supply a market for 'healing' stones, whereas the stones you collect yourself can be imbued with healing properties.

✵ Not buying unnecessary things made from non-replenishable resources.

✵ Taking our litter away with us and disposing of it thoughtfully. This includes not leaving candle wax, dead flowers, etc., at stone circles or other sacred sites, or burying items there. Don't change the site, let the site change you.

✵ Not throwing things away which could be passed on to friends or given to a charity shop.

✵ Using recycling facilities.

✵ Thinking carefully about the way we keep and treat our pets and animals. This is not to say that your cat should not be house-trained or that your dog should be allowed to bite, rather that you should think twice before making them perform foolish tricks just because you want to appear clever. It also means making sure that you provide the animals in your care with the best environment for them to live as normal as life as possible. Keeping a snake in a tank or a bird in a cage may be fashionable, but does it show any respect for the creature?

✵ Making appropriate protest when we feel that unnecessary damage is being done to the environment – and not just because we don't want

something in our neighbourhood. Deciding what is appropriate protest can be quite difficult, but it is worth remembering that protests made with enough support, at the right time to the right people, through the formal system, are more likely to succeed than something newsworthy just as the bulldozers move in. A lot of publicity at that late a stage will not save a lost cause! Remember, politicians count one well-written letter as representing the views of 100 people.

FREEDOM OF SPIRITUAL CHOICE

We believe that everyone is entitled to their own spiritual beliefs, so long as they harm no one else. This means that people are entitled to practise whatever they believe is right for them as a religion, spirituality or faith, as long as they do not harm anyone else or use any kind of force or coercion to persuade others to take up those beliefs. Witchcraft is a non-proselytizing religion, which means we do not seek converts. Speaking personally, that means I am quite happy to explain what I believe and what I do, and if you choose to read this book that is your choice, but I would not force you to do so.

Witches do not feel that it is necessary to change the way other people approach their version of the divine, nor that it is important to be one of a large number of others all believing the same thing. Other faiths do not always feel this way and many seek to change the way those outside their faith believe. They seek converts, believing that theirs is the 'one true faith', and to this end they preach to the young, often from pre-school age onwards. They will frequently express as fact beliefs which are a part of their faith.

However, part of allowing everyone to follow their own beliefs is the concept of informed choice. Hence Witches prefer to encourage their children

to examine many belief systems objectively, fostering questioning and discussion. I would not prevent my child from attending, for example, a church, although I know of few other religions whose members would be prepared to find out what happens at a Wiccan festival, let alone allow their young to attend.

PERSONAL RESPONSIBILITY

We believe that what you say and do is your own responsibility. We believe this is true for everyone – although we do not force people (or even expect them) to believe the same. You can blame no outside agency – whether the Devil or your parents! – for making you behave the way you do.

Whilst we are all, to a certain extent, conditioned by what has happened to us in the past, once we reach the age where we can think for ourselves, we have the choice and ability to change our behaviour in our future. To do this we must first of all understand ourselves and what makes us react the way we do. Say you come from a background where physical punishment (for example smacking) was used to deter bad behaviour, it is possible that this is the way you will react when your own children are naughty, but you can choose not to react in this way. If on the last two occasions you told your friend a secret they let it out and you had a fight, you can choose to avoid this next time by not telling your friend, rather than blaming them for being loose-tongued. If you drink too much alcohol and do something stupid you cannot blame the drink – *you* drank it. All these are elements of personal responsibility.

Another aspect of this is taking responsibility for the effect you have on other people – but only so far as your responsibility goes. As an example, if you are in a relationship with someone who is very attached to you, but you no longer feel strongly for them, then obviously your responsibility is to end the relationship. If you take to heart the Wiccan Rede, then you will do so as gently as possible, without causing unnecessary pain, whilst still being as honest as you can. However, if that person then runs off and joins the army and gets killed in action, whilst it is natural to feel some guilt, that is not your personal responsibility. Their feelings and subsequent actions are their personal responsibilities. Choosing to do what is right for yourself regardless of how others may feel at first seems very harsh. But it is an important part of personal responsibility to be personally honest and in the long term it does a lot less harm than pretending to be someone you are not or to feel something you do not.

Furthermore, personal responsibility includes knowing when not to get involved in the affairs of others. Imagine that your best friend has split up with her partner and comes to you with a tale of woe, telling you how badly he treated her. Of course you can sympathize and comfort her, but what you should not do is then rush round to everyone you know spreading stories about what a nasty person he is and how he should be avoided. First, you only know one side of the story and however honest you think your friend is, her perceptions will be coloured by her feelings, especially in the heat of the moment. Secondly, whatever happened in their relationship is their personal responsibility, not yours. Your responsibility as a friend involves being there for your friend, not in being everywhere else and stirring up everyone else. This is very hard to achieve, especially when someone close to you feels seriously offended, but wisdom often lies in doing less, not more.

THE WICCAN REDE

One of the ways in which personal responsibility is emphasized is through the Wiccan Rede. This is the rule that Witches strive to follow and by which they measure their actions. As mentioned before, it is a positive morality, rather than a set of 'don'ts' or 'shalt nots'. The Rede comes in many forms, some poetic, some lengthy, but however it is expressed, it always contains the same key phrase at its heart: <u>'An' it harm none, do what thou will.'</u> This rather archaic phrasing (often modernized to 'And it harm none, do what you will') simply means that you should do what is right for you in your life, but that in doing so you should try not to hurt others. Now obviously there are times when doing what is personally right will almost certainly hurt someone else, but here you are required to make your own moral judgement – to consider, accept and live with the consequences.

PERSONAL DEVELOPMENT

As a Witch, you are also responsible for your own personal development, for fulfilling your own potential. This means continuing your development throughout your life. It may mean taking up some form of adult education, whether to make up for opportunities lost or to set out in a new direction. If you find yourself headed in a direction which is wrong for you, then you are responsible for changing course! It does mean working at obtaining all the skills that you need to make your life as fulfilled as possible. Above all it means that if you decide on the path of the Witch, you are responsible for learning and growing on that path. You cannot expect others to do it for you or to you. You must seek the teacher(s), you must ask the questions and you must expect to set the pace.

In the Craft this means that you will need to choose the specialities you wish to learn, find the books and set your own time scale for taking on new knowledge and skills. You may not find the 'right' teacher for some time after you have made the decision to walk this path, so it is up to you to start work immediately. Many believe that the teacher does not appear until the student is ready.

If, in time, you do find a group or Coven to work with, the High Priestess will not tell you what to learn and when. She will not give you any more help than you ask for and she will certainly not do the work for you. If you seek to learn she will guide you in your studies, but she will expect you to be the driving force.

WE ARE EACH OUR OWN PRIEST OR PRIESTESS

Linked to this is the belief that every individual has the right and the ability to communicate with the divine for themselves, that we do not need an intermediary to intercede or interpret our Gods and Goddesses for us. We do not need a specialist 'priestly caste' to tell us who, what, why, how and when to worship, as we are capable of making these decisions for ourselves.

THE ELEMENTS

The ancients believed that all nature was made up from the elements of Earth, Air, Fire and Water. Witches believe that these elements, together with the fifth element of Spirit, make up ourselves and the world around us. We believe that these elements are very real energies which we can access by

understanding the way that they work within us and around us. The elements represent different aspects of our being: Earth is our physical selves, our flesh, blood and bones; Air is our thoughts; Fire is our passions and enthusiasms; Water our emotions; Spirit is the force or energy which is ourselves.

The five energies are represented in the pentacle which is worn by many Witches and which often appears on the Altar at rituals. The idea that the reversed, upside-down pentacle is linked to Satanism has its roots in Hollywood and popular fiction. In the UK and elsewhere, the reversed pentacle indicates the Horned God, the male aspect of fertility, or in some traditions the second-degree Witch.

The elements are also linked to the points of the compass and the seasons of the year. They have colours, sounds, scents, flowers, animals, birds and trees ascribed to them, as well as many other links which are often referred to as correspondences. There are correspondences for almost everything including the signs of the Zodiac, the days of the week and the hours of the day. They are often used in Magical workings, both in the Craft and in other Magical traditions, to help to achieve results. The Traditional Craft does not rely so much upon them as some other paths.

To understand how correspondences work it can help to think of this in terms of rowing up a river. If the wind, current and tide are all in your favour, you will make faster and easier progress than if one or more is against you. Even if all those things are against you, you can still reach your destination, it will just require more effort and strength. Similarly, if you use candles, cloths, oils and incense related to the element with which you are working, then you may find it easier to gain the desired result. The use of correspondences, however, will not make up for lack of focus, practice and ability.

THE SABBATS AND WHEEL OF THE YEAR

Witches celebrate eight seasonal festivals or Sabbats:

Samhain, 31 October. The beginning and therefore end of the Pagan year. The time when the Goddess returns as the Crone or Wise One.

Yule, the Winter Solstice, 21 December. The time when the days begin to lengthen and the rebirth of the Sun is celebrated.

Imbolg, 2 February. The time when the first buds are seen on the trees; the return of the Goddess as the Maiden.

Oestara, the Spring Equinox, 21 March. The time when day and night are equal. A time of balance and of throwing out the old and taking on the new.

Beltane, 1 May. The time when the marriage of the Goddess and the God is celebrated. The Goddess becomes the Mother and the God returns to reign beside her.

Litha, the Summer Solstice, 21 June. The height of the Sun King's power, when the days begin to shorten again.

Lammas, 1 August. The time when the first harvest is brought in; the feast of the sacrificial God.

Madron, the Autumn Equinox, 21 September. Again day and night are equal and again this is a time of balance. This is the height of the harvest and a time of returning things to the way they should be.

Taken together these are often referred to as the Wheel of the Year, for, like a wheel, the cycle is never-ending, starting again as soon as it finishes.

The Sabbats celebrate the changing seasons of the old agricultural year as well as the festivals and lives of the Goddess and the God. As with the elements, we also see the meaning of the Sabbats in our daily lives and use the energies of the cycle to work towards understanding and balance for ourselves and for those around us. The Sabbats are often seen as a time of celebration. However, there is much successful Magic that can be worked on these occasions. (There is much more on these festivals and the Wheel of the Year in Chapter 4, 'The Eight Sabbats'.)

THE CYCLE OF THE MOON

Just as the Wheel of the Year expresses the yearly cycle, so the phases of the Moon give us a monthly cycle. In these phases (often called aspects) we see a repeating cycle of the Goddess. Witches believe that the Goddess has three aspects: Maiden, Mother and Crone (or Wise One). These three aspects are reflected in all things, for everything has the same three phases of beginning, completeness (or fruitfulness) and rest.

In the cycle of the Moon, the role of the God is primarily that of Consort, although throughout a year of Moons, many are attributed to the God so that the cycle of the Goddess exists within that of the God. Again we see the reference to balance, for each depends upon the other to create the whole, just as in any partnership. (See the next chapter for more on the worship of the Goddess and the God, the way that the cycle of the Moon operates in our lives and the way that Witches utilize that cycle in their workings.)

MAGIC

Witches believe in and practise Magic. This is not the 'magic' of stage conjuring but a very real force which can be used to make changes in our lives and in the lives of those around us. It has been said that Magic is 'the ability to make change by force of will' and this is a very good working definition.

Healing is one of the forms of Magic for which Witches are most frequently asked. Many people who otherwise would say that they do not believe in the Craft will seek healing for themselves and their near and dear, whether for physical ills or for emotional support, perhaps after a bereavement.

Other kinds of Magic I find commonly requested include:

⭐ Work-related Magic – how to find a job, be successful at interview or to gain a promotion or pay rise.

⭐ Magic for help in studying or examinations.

⭐ Relationship Magic – to reunite those who have parted, to heal arguments, to gain the affections of someone new (often referred to as 'love Magic') or even to drive off a persistent unwanted admirer.

⭐ Protection or defensive Magic, for people who feel under threat in some way, whether physical or psychic. This can also include people who feel there are 'bad' influences at work in their house, car or workplace. This is a quite common impression, although quite often it is the relationships in life which cause the bad atmosphere rather than anything else.

Any kind of Magical working needs a good deal of thought. One of the sayings of the Craft is 'Be careful what you wish for'. In considering whether or not to work Magic you have to be aware of the potential outcomes of what you are asking. Seeking success in an interview may give you a job which you subsequently hate, asking for money may result in you inheriting it from a loved one. Love Magic is probably the most treacherous of all. Initially most people will argue that they do not care whether the desired one is attracted by Magic or not, but later they will find that knowing that someone only loves them because of a spell, not because of who they really are, can destroy self-confidence and self-esteem far more than not being able to gain the object of their desires in the first place.

When working Magic you have to be certain that you work the kind of spell which will cure the problem and not one which will make things worse in the long term. You also have to realize that sometimes events may seem to work against us, but perhaps the Goddess knows best. A very real example of this is the case of someone who set their heart on buying a particular car. When all the usual avenues of borrowing money to buy it did not work, they worked Magic to obtain the money. Within a couple of days their final loan request was granted and they were able to buy the car. A good result, you might think. However, shortly afterwards their circumstances changed, leaving them without work and making it much harder to repay the money they had borrowed. In addition, the tax and insurance on this particular model have since been increased and the value of the car has fallen, meaning that should they sell it there will not be enough money to repay the remainder of the amount they borrowed.

Magic is one of the things which, at first sight, makes Witchcraft different from many other faiths. However, we have more in common with other beliefs than many people realize and the use of Magic takes many forms. Is the power of prayer so very different from Magic? (Chapter 6, 'Magic', and Chapter 7, 'Spellcraft and Herb Lore', will tell you more about this fascinating and complex subject.)

THE LAW OF THREEFOLD RETURN

The Law of Threefold Return, often called the 'Rule of Three' states: 'Whatever you do, be it good or ill, will be returned to you threefold.' So if you perform benevolent Magic, good things will come your way, while if you perform negative Magic, bad things will happen to you. There is some debate between members of the Craft as to whether the Rule of Three is really a part of traditional Witchcraft or whether it has been added in recent years, perhaps in order to make people think carefully about the Magic they are about to perform. However, whether or not you feel that there is a historical basis for the Rule of Three, certainly there is no harm in giving careful thought to the justification and consequences of any Magic (or for that matter any non-Magical action) you are about to perform. If you are not prepared for your actions to be returned to you three times over, then perhaps you should be considering alternative actions.

In my experience, and the experience of many other Witches, any Magical action does have consequences for the person who performs it and the greater the Magic, the greater the consequences. Many believe that this is because the universe is finite and if you take from one place there will be a price to be paid in another.

DIVINATION

Divination is the ability to find out things which might otherwise be hidden, whether that be the past, present, future or the presence of water or precious metals or minerals. It can be practised with or without tools such as the tarot, crystal ball, runes, tea-leaves or dowsing rods. It is referred to by many names, including fortune-telling, psychic reading, dowsing, etc., although Witches will often use the somewhat older term of scrying. Nearly all Witches practise some form of divination. It is not a way of conjuring spirits who will answer questions, rather a way of accessing the inner mind.

As with healing Magic, divination is something which is frequently asked of Witches. People want to know not only what is going to happen, but also what is happening in the world around them. What they generally want is the ability to take charge of their lives and affect their 'Fate'. Learning to scry is not, however, as simple as buying a deck of cards or pouch of runes and learning the meanings by heart. In order to be of use to the enquirer you need to be able to relate the meaning of what you see to the life of the person you are reading for. You will also need to be able to present options to them, so that they can alter their behaviour to take advantage of favourable circumstances or avoid potential problems. Much of what you see during a reading may relate to the personality of the person before you and this may involve highlighting some of their bad habits or traits, together with advising them on how to change these. In this way a reputable reader becomes much more like a counsellor, or the parent aspect of the definition we started out with. Unfortunately there are many less than reputable readers about and it is difficult to tell the difference without either personal experience or the recommendation of a friend whose judgement you trust.

The best known traditional forms of divination are:

★ *Tarot* This is a special deck of cards which has five suits instead of the four found in playing cards. There are over 200 tarot decks on the market at present of varying shapes, sizes, themes and even number of cards, although 78 is most common. For a reading a number of cards are laid out in a pattern, called a spread, and their the combination and progression are interpreted. The tarot is especially useful for readings where a high level of counselling is needed.

★ *Runes* Runes can be made from wood, stone, pottery or other materials. Each rune has a different symbol on it and it is the interpretation of the combinations of symbols which gives the starting-point for the reading. Most rune sets are Norse in origin and their meaning can seem somewhat

obscure unless you are familiar with Nordic traditions and their
historic context.

★ *Crystal ball* In this form of divination a sphere or rounded shape of glass,
crystal or other gemstone is used. The reader does not see images as such
in the ball, but uses it to focus their inner mind on the person or question
in front of them.

★ *Palmistry* Palm readers interpret the lines on both hands to determine the
character and/or future of the person who seeks the reading. Palmistry is
particularly good for identifying skills and talents, whether inborn or
acquired.

★ *Dowsing* For dowsing, various tools, including sticks, metal rods and
pendulums, are used, usually to locate something, either in the ground or
sometimes on a map. The most frequent use of dowsing is to locate water
and many dowsers are employed by local water companies or farmers for
this purpose.

★ *Tea-leaves* Reading tea-leaves is a very old skill, which has largely died out
since the tea bag has become popular. For a reading, tea is made in a pot.
It is not strained and once a cup of it has been drunk, the residue left in
the cup is used to make an interpretation of events, usually forthcoming.
Tea-leaf readings are still as valid a method today as they have ever been,
even if the skill of drinking unstrained tea has been largely lost!

★ *Astrology* Astrology is not simply another method of divination or scrying,
although it can be used to predict events. True astrology, rather than the
horoscopes you see in the papers, which deal only with generalizations
regarding Sun signs, is both a science and an art. The science lies in

calculating the positions of all of the planets at the time of birth. The information thus gathered is put together in what is known as a natal chart. The art lies in interpreting the chart to give an accurate picture of the personality, skills and abilities of the person concerned. When done skilfully, this enables the subject to gain self-understanding and the ability to maximize their potential. Like other methods of divination, the practice of astrology is not limited to Witches – people from many belief systems use such techniques.

✭ *Psychic readings* All those who divine, or 'read', are to a greater or lesser extent psychic, but a psychic reader generally does not use any of the tools of divination to aid them in their reading. A clairvoyant is another term for a psychic reader. The word 'clairvoyant' simply means 'to see clearly'.

Psychics should not be confused with mediums, who are those who use contacts in the spirit world to obtain their information. This is not a form of scrying or divination. Whilst a person may be both a psychic and a medium, the two skills are different. Witches do not believe that it is right to summon back the spirits of those who have gone before, whether to tell the future or for any other reason.

Witches may use any of the above techniques of scrying or they may use methods which are less known outside the Craft:

✭ *The Dark Mirror* This can be either a watch glass coated with soot (although many Witches prefer to use the rather less messy medium of paint) or a bowl of water into which black dye or ink has been added. In both cases the resulting black reflective surface is used in much the same way as a crystal ball.

✶ *Fire* Here either the flames themselves are consulted or in some cases the hot embers are used. In the days when living fires (and large fireplaces) were common, many Witches would leave a piece of wood or corn from the harvest in the fireplace close to the flames. This would burn slowly overnight and the ashes would be interpreted next morning.

✶ *The Witches' runes* Unlike the runes themselves, which are comprised of 20 or so pieces, the Witches' runes have only eight pieces and the symbols on them are more pictorial. Their interpretation, whilst initially simpler, requires a greater study of the Craft.

There are many other methods of divination in use today, from the interpretation of the residue in a beer glass to some very costly kits and card decks sold in stores around the world. In actual fact almost anything can be used for scrying. The secret is to find the method which suits you and your pocket. Not everyone finds every method easy to master and most people try several before deciding on the one they feel at home with. It is also important to remember that expensive is not necessarily better. You can spend a seriously large amount of money on a tarot deck, but it will not give you a better reading than a cheap one, and quite often the runes you make yourself will work better for you than the ones which came in a velvet pouch with a special reading board and cloth.

REINCARNATION AND THE SUMMERLANDS

Witches believe in reincarnation, that we return to this world many times over. We also believe that after death we move firstly to the Summerlands, a place where we may rest and become renewed. In the Summerlands we may be able to meet those we have loved who have gone before us and we can choose the lessons that we will learn in our next life.

However, belief in reincarnation does not allow us to be complacent about the life we are currently living. You can neither blame your current problems on things that may or may not have happened in a previous existence, nor can you simply postpone dealing with current problems in the hope that next time around things will be better. Whether you believe in reincarnation or not, one thing is certain: you will only get one chance at this life and it is up to you to make the best of it. This is something which needs to be borne in mind should you feel the temptation to explore your past lives, whether through meditation or any other technique. Whilst there are often many interesting or useful things that can be learned from past-life recall, a few people do find the subject so fascinating that they neglect to make the most of their current life. As with all things, balance should be sought.

THREE

MOON WORSHIP?

As addressed earlier, one of the misconceptions about the Craft is that Witches worship the Moon. This is not so, though the Moon is significant to Witches because the phases of the Moon represent the aspects of the Goddess and because her consort, the God, is always with her. Witches utilize those phases in their worship and their working by timing their rituals and Magic to coincide with the phases of the Moon to which they will be most attuned.

The Moon orbits the Earth, taking just over 28 days to complete its circuit. Whilst this happens the Earth orbits the Sun, taking just over 365 days to complete its circuit, and the Earth rotates on its own axis once every 24 or so hours. Bear in mind that none of these figures is precise. Time is an invention of man, not a natural or scientific law, and was created out of the need to explain these natural phenomena. As a result of all these movements, the Moon we see from Earth rises and sets at different times and in different parts of the sky and because of the relative positions of the Sun, Moon and Earth, it appears to change its shape. It waxes from a thin crescent to full circle, then wanes to a thin crescent again and finally disappears from the sky altogether for a few days before repeating the cycle. As the apparent size of the Moon changes, so does its influence on the Earth, and this is most clearly seen in its effects upon the tides. This influence can also be seen to affect humans, not surprisingly as we are mostly made of water. For women this link is easy to see in their monthly cycle, but everyone, male or female, is subject to monthly fluctuations in energy, patience, the ability to concentrate, and so on. These are often referred to as biorhythms.

Early peoples from every civilization and every part of the world have, or had, stories to explain these changes in the Moon. All of these have certain threads in common. The Moon grows, bringing promise and strength. It reaches fullness, representing fertility and fruitfulness. It declines and then enters a resting, or hidden, phase before starting again. In the Craft these stages in the Moon's cycle are linked to the three aspects of the Goddess. In some other belief systems the Lunar cycle is linked to the stories of the God. However, legends of the Triple Goddess can be found from almost all civilizations and all parts of the globe. Although some mythologies will give different names to the different aspects of the Goddess, it is important to remember that they are all aspects or faces of the one Goddess. The Triple Goddess is Maiden, Mother and Crone (or Wise One), and we have to put aside some of our modern prejudices when we look at these terms, for

Maiden need not mean young in years and Crone certainly does not mean past her useful life!

The Maiden is youthful. She represents fresh starts and new beginnings, enthusiasm and energy. In times past she would be seen as any woman who had commenced puberty but who had not yet given birth to a child. The New Moon represents the Maiden and it is at this time of the month that we prefer to work Magic directed towards new growth or anything which is being started. It is the time to draw things towards us. So we would ask for help in starting a new project or job, or to acquire new skills. On a practical level it is a good time to sow seeds or start new plants.

The Mother is more mature. She represents fertility and fruitfulness, nurturing and caring. Her image is maternal, someone who has had a child (or children) and is in the process of raising them. The Full Moon represents the Mother and this is the time of month when our Magic is directed towards healing, nurturing and protecting. At this time Magic is performed for the healing of physical, emotional and mental illness, both for ourselves and for others.

The Crone is the Wise One. She represents knowledge and understanding. In times past this was the woman who had finished raising her family, whose experience of life and observation of the people around her had given her the knowledge and skill to know those things which were not obvious to others. The later stages of the Waning Moon represent the Crone and this is the time when Magic is worked towards knowledge and understanding, and when divination is most likely to be successful. This is also the time for the banishing of things such as bad habits, old guilt, poor self-image. The Crone is also the one who presides over death, the time of rest after labours, and, because the cycle of life, death and rebirth is never-ending, she also prepares the way for new birth and the Maiden. Death is something we are accustomed to turn away from, but in the context of the Craft, its place in the cycle is necessary to allow new things to start.

The few days when there is no visible Moon every month are called the Dark of the Moon. It is often considered that these nights, when the Goddess is hiding her face, are a time when no Magic should be performed. This is not strictly true, but working at the Dark of the Moon is something which should really be kept for emergencies and for when you are fully in tune with the energies in the ebb and flow of the Moon, otherwise you may find yourself working many times harder than is actually necessary, and with uncertain results. If you practise the Craft regularly for long enough you will know when you are ready to work at the Dark of the Moon. You will also come to learn that there are very few Magics that cannot wait a day or so until the New Moon rises to lend her youthful energy to your purpose.

So far I have referred to the cycle of the Moon only in terms of the Goddess, however we must remember that the God is of equal importance. He does not change in the same way with the phases of the Moon. His role is that of consort or partner and he remains constantly at the Goddess's side, changing little throughout the course of the month, although in a year of Moons there are some that are directly linked to the God. For example the Hunter's Moon, which is the one nearest to Samhain and the 'largest' Moon of the year, is related to the God as he moves into his aspect of Leader of the Wild Hunt. The aspects of the God are seen more clearly through the cycle or Wheel of the Year, where the Goddess sometimes appears to take a less obvious role. However, both the Goddess and the God are worshipped equally in both the Lunar and the annual cycles. It may be useful to think of this in terms of two equal partners, only one of whom can speak at a time. The non-speaker may appear to take a lesser role, but in reality it is simply the fact that their partner is the one doing the talking which makes them seem to be more prominent at that time.

Witches refer to the Goddess and the God by a large number of different names and also as the Goddess and the God or the Lord and Lady. For many people this causes some confusion, for how can you believe in one deity but have a number of names? Earlier I used the analogy of a mirror ball, with each facet an aspect of the divine, known by a different name. On a more human scale, think about an individual, we'll call her Ann. Ann is someone's daughter, someone's sister, wife to her husband, mother to her children. Ann also has a job; to those she supervises she is 'boss', to those she reports to she is a worker and to her customers she shows a different aspect yet again. Each of these roles will bring out a different facet of Ann and she may well be seen as almost a different person by all these different people, but she is still just the one Ann. At some point in Ann's life her parents will die and at this time her role of daughter will reduce until it is almost forgotten, or she may give up work and those working roles will reduce, but should she start work again, they can quickly be revived. Individual Gods and Goddesses may likewise 'fall into disuse' but if their worship is revived, then their strength will grow again. For, like each of Ann's roles, the Goddesses and Gods have personalities which can stand alone and which grow in strength if called upon more often.

The Gods and Goddesses known to Witches today come from a variety of pantheons and from a variety of times and lands. Knowledge of these deities has been spread by conquerors, invaders and immigrants throughout history and with today's global communication that knowledge is easily shared all around the world. So you may find that Witches in America, England and Australia share the same deities, though they may follow a completely differ-ent pantheon from those in a neighbouring town.

There is no way I can give a comprehensive list of Goddesses and Gods, their stories or their roles here, but the following are just a few to give you an introduction.

PERSEPHONE, DEMETER AND HECATE

This is just one example of the Triple Goddess. The story of Persephone's abduction by Pluto, Lord of the Underworld, is well known in its modern form but it is well worth researching the fuller tale, including the role of Hecate, who is the third aspect or Crone, and who is often called the Witches' Goddess.

ISIS, OSIRIS, NEPTHYS AND SET

These four Egyptian Goddesses and Gods are perhaps the best known of the Egyptian pantheon. Their story is one of those which have been changed and reinterpreted so that the 'villains' seem all bad and the 'heroes' all good. However, the full story is much more complex and contains all the ingredients of a soap opera! Nepthys is often invoked as a healer, particularly in more complicated or serious cases.

VENUS AND APHRODITE

Originally these were two quite different Goddesses. The Romans were the first to confuse their Goddess Venus with the Greek Aphrodite and both have come to represent love and beauty. Venus is often invoked by Witches who wish to work Magic for forms of self-love such as increased self-respect or personal emotional healing.

CERIDWYN

In the story of this Welsh Celtic Goddess, she devours Gwion, who has stolen the potion of inspiration which she has brewed in her Magical cauldron, and gives birth to the great poet and bard Taliesin. Ceridwyn, like Hecate, is also referred to as a Witches' Goddess.

CERNUNNOS

This Celtic God of the Hunt is one of several Gods often shown wearing antlers. Whilst his mythology is somewhat vague, a horned or antlered God is one of the older Gods of northern Europe.

THOR, ODIN, FREYA, FRIG AND LOKI

These Scandinavian Gods and Goddesses and many others share a vast mythology which is often referred to as the Northern Tradition. Whilst this tradition has much in common with Witchcraft, it is often considered to be a different path.

ENKI, INANNA, ERISKEGAL AND DUMUZI

The Sumerian Goddess Inanna is another, like Persephone, who descends to the Underworld, in this case ruled over by her sister Eriskegal. Again mourning falls upon the world until she is rescued by her father Enki. Her husband, Dumuzi, who has betrayed her, is sent to take her place. The story of Inanna is just one of many which tell us of the Descent of the Goddess, a tale which is very important in understanding the Craft and which features strongly in certain forms of initiation.

This, as I have said, is just a small selection of Goddesses and Gods, and there are many, many more. It is well worth spending some time reading up on them and their legends, for these tales give us the knowledge to select those we feel we can best work with. For example it is only when you know the role of Nepthys in the healing of Osiris that you understand why she is considered helpful in difficult cases. Also, our interpretation of Gods is often coloured by their appearance in modern productions. Anubis, for example, often appears in horror stories as a God of Death. But the ancient Egyptians believed that as the guardian of the gates of life and death, his role was as much to prevent people passing through too early as to speed them on their way when the time was right. For this reason his statue was often placed by the bed of a child as a protector.

Most Witches have their 'favourite' deity or deities. These will be the ones with whom they most closely identify and may even be the ones to whom they dedicate themselves and their Witchcraft. These Gods and/or Goddesses may come from one pantheon or from a mixture, but it is usual to stay within any one pantheon during the course of any one working and not mix, say, a Greek Goddess with a Celtic God, as these deities will not necessarily be in sympathy with each other and the energies they produce may cancel each other out. In any case it is not necessary to 'mix and match' in this way as, with a little effort, you can usually discover the name of the appropriate 'partner' within the same pantheon.

As almost all the information about the divine has been handed down since before the days of written history, or in some cases written in a form we cannot fully understand, such as hieroglyphs, there is often more than one way to spell any individual's name, although one spelling may have become more accepted than others. Additionally, some quite different Gods or

Goddesses may have very similar names. These are both reasons why familiarity with their roles and stories is important, so that you know exactly whom you are talking to.

Many Goddesses and Gods have a non-human form, usually in addition to their human one. This may be animal, as in the case of Arachne, Greek Goddess of weavers, who takes the form of a spider. Those of you who are afraid of spiders may find it interesting to know that meditating on the story of Arachne and making an offering to her (I usually suggest making a small spider by tying four lengths of thread together eight times at their centres and placing it in a tree) is often a large step towards overcoming arachnaphobia. Alternatively, the form of the God or Goddess might be that of a mythological creature, such as the Hydra, or may be part-human, part-'beast', as in the case of the Goat-Footed God Pan.

Many Witches like to have an image of the Goddess and the God on their Altar when working Magic and even just around the house generally. This can be a statue, a picture or drawing, or some other symbol. One of the easiest ways to do this is to purchase a postcard from a museum or copy an illustration from a book. If you wish to imbue your image with your own personal power it is a good idea to put at least some of the creative effort in yourself, perhaps making a statue or making the frame for a picture. Where the deity has an alternate form, like Arachne's spider, the image may be of that form. It is not necessary to have an image of each and every Goddess or God you wish to work with, but it can be very helpful to have something around which aids your focus.

Witches do not always refer to the Goddess and the God by any name at all. Some prefer only to talk about the Goddess and the God, or even to refer to them as the Lady and the Lord. In this case the images they may keep around them may be fairly simple – a round stone with a hole through it to represent the Goddess, a phallically shaped stone to represent the God, for example. Of course, two things which represent the Goddess and the God and which are present at most rituals are the Chalice and the Athame (the Witches' knife).

There are many reasons for wishing to have symbols of your deities around you. Perhaps the most important is so that you have a memory key. It is easier, especially at first, if you have a tangible object to focus on, rather than working purely on the mental/psychic plane. It works in much the same way as a mnemonic does, so that when you look at the image it becomes easier to remember all the attributes that you have associated with it.

However, obtaining an image of the Goddess and/or the God is only a small step in learning to worship and work with them. As I said earlier, you will need a good understanding of their personalities, roles and stories, and for this you will need first to read up on them and secondly to make personal contact. To those who have been brought up within one of the 'orthodox' patriarchal religions this may at first sound quite impossible – after all, that is what priests are there for in those religions. However, in the Craft we are each our own Priest or Priestess and need no intermediary to intercede with our Gods for us. We are able to make direct contact and gain personal experience of the divine.

The simplest and most effective way of meeting and coming to know the Goddess and the God is through meditation. However, meditation itself is not always easy to master and for that reason I recommend a technique of guided meditation known as Pathworking. In meditation you are required to focus either on a single point or on nothingness; in Pathworking you follow a storyline which leads you to a point at which your subconscious mind can take over. You can find written or recorded Pathworkings for sale, or you can write your own. If you choose to do the latter you will need to spend some time making sure that you have an acceptable storyline which will lead you to an environment which is compatible with your view of the Goddess or God you wish to meet and which causes you no personal concern. It is no good deciding to go on a journey to meet Hermes at the top of a mountain if you have a fear of heights! Even though a Pathworking may feel as if it is all taking place 'in your head', it is in fact the first introduction to working on the psychic plane, where fear and doubt are as great (if not greater) distractions as in everyday life.

Some individuals prefer to write their Pathworking down so that they can work on it in detail before committing it to memory. Others like to write it out and record it for their own use. The third option is to decide on the outline and then fill the detail in as you go on the journey.

The following will give you an idea of how a Pathworking might work:

Find a time and a place where you will be uninterrupted and make yourself comfortable. You will not be able to concentrate if, for example, you are too cold, worried about being disturbed, or if your clothes are cutting into you.

Imagine yourself going on a walk through the woods. Decide whether it is day or night, what season it is, whether it is warm or cold, windy or sunny. Take note of the trees, flowers and animals around you. Take your time to fill in the detail, not only of what you see, but also of the sounds and scents around you. Give some thought to what you are wearing, whether you have shoes on, a coat, or even a cloak. Make sure you are comfortably settled in this environment before moving on in your journey to the meeting with whoever you have decided you wish to meet.

Decide on the environment they will be in. Perhaps it will be Ceridwyn with her cauldron. Will she be in the open or will you have to enter a house or even a cave? Give a lot of thought to the detail of this. What will she look like and be wearing? Will you speak first or will she greet you and invite you in? Do you have a question for her, or are you just there to see what she may say to you, or even give to you?

When you are sure that your meeting is over, be sure to thank her. Then retrace your steps to the start of your journey. Make sure that all the time you are doing this that you pay attention to the detail all around you, as often the most important clues are those which crop up along the way, and they may be symbolic. Anything which seems out of place to you or which feels to have more importance than its appearance would normally warrant should be taken note of.

When you are sure your journey is over, sit up and make a few notes about what you have seen. The notes are quite important, for in the same way that a dream fades on waking, often the detail of a Pathworking may fade away quickly.

The first few times you do this you may feel as though this is all taking place in your imagination or that you are only seeing the things which you have thought up and placed into the story. But you will find that after a bit of practice images come to your mind without you actually having to think them up and these images will seem just as real as 'real life'. You will also find that characters may enter the 'story' without you having to imagine them in any way and these characters may speak to you or show you things which you do not expect to see. This is all part of developing the ability to work on the psychic level. Some people think that these images are placed there by the Goddess or the God, others consider that you are simply learning to understand and interpret your own subconscious mind. Either way, there is no doubt that the things you see, hear, feel and experience during these meditations can be useful in your everyday waking life, although their meanings often take a bit of work to understand.

Many of the things you experience in meditation will be symbolic. Sometimes you will come across their meaning through reading or research, at other times you may have to take the information on trust and wait for its meaning to become clear in time. However, one of the most important things you will have to learn to do is to trust your intuition. On the whole, things that feel good and right *are* good and right. Interpretations which feel wrong, perhaps selfish or the outcome you are hoping for, are usually those which you are trying to read into the mystery. This is where you have to train your self-knowledge to the point where you can be honest with yourself about your intentions. Once you know what your hopes are, you can analyse the results with a more open mind, because the right interpretation may not necessarily be the one you wished for. Conversely, once you know your fears, you are better able to dismiss interpretations which arise directly from those fears.

You also need to be aware that sometimes the real interpretation is a lot less complicated than you were expecting. If you meet the Goddess on your Pathworking and she smiles at you and you feel welcome, being welcome to the Goddess may be all the interpretation that is required.

The meaning may also have its roots in the mundane world rather than the mystic. To give an example, a young mother came to me asking for my interpretation of her dream. She had dreamt that all her teeth fell out and on looking it up in a book, she found that this was an omen of death. She was very upset and worried as she neither wanted her daughter to die nor to die herself and leave her daughter without a mother. Her fears were obviously of death, but the reality was a lot simpler. I simply asked her if she had missed a dental appointment and on finding she had, it was not difficult to point out the meaning of her dream! This highlights the need to consider more than one interpretation. Whilst the one you think of first is often the correct one, you do need to check that you are not allowing your judgement to be coloured in any way.

It also highlights a very common misinterpretation – people tend to take visions of death, or even the Death card in the tarot, literally. However, death is very rarely foretold, as it is not given to most of us to know. In tarot, the Death card usually appears when there is a major change ahead, when the death of one thing leads to the start of another. For example, a person approaching their wedding is preparing for the death of their single life, which will lead to the birth of their married life. Also, be very wary of relying on someone else's interpretation, especially if you are taking it from a book, as your experience is unlikely to be identical to the author's.

Meditation and Pathworking are not just techniques which we use to understand the Goddess and the God, but also to discover more about the elements, to answer questions and to understand the world around us. These techniques can also be used to prepare ourselves for everyday situations – an interview, returning faulty goods to a store and any number of 'confrontational' situations where you feel that a bit of private practice might help. In this kind of case your journey will be based very much on the circumstances you are expecting to meet in the 'real' world.

There is one other major way to discover the Goddess and the God in addition to reading or meditation, and that is to look for them in the world around you. You can see the aspects of the Goddess through the phases of the Moon and it is well worth taking the time to find out when these are so that you can at least look outside to her.

You can also see the effects of Maiden, Mother and Crone in the growth of plants and trees, which show the cycles of life, death and rebirth clearly. Watch for the aspects of the God as Hunter and Hunted in the life of wild animals and birds, for often you will see his roles change; the cat hunting birds becomes hunted by the dog. Nature often seems very cruel to us, especially when we see the results of the hunt, but it is worth remembering that in nature it is the weak and the sick which are usually taken, and often given release from pain and suffering, thereby ensuring that the rest of the herd or breed remains healthy. You do not have to go far to see this in action – our televisions show the cycle of life, death and new life in the natural world.

However, if you can get out and observe at first hand it is far better.

You can also see intimations of the divine in the most 'unnatural' things. For example, buildings go up, have useful lives, are abandoned and decay, the land rests and something new begins. Products are launched, become popular and then outlive their usefulness, only to be relaunched in a new format. By looking at the world in this way you can come to an understanding of the roles of the Goddess and the God and to a greater understanding of your own place in it.

FOUR

THE EIGHT SABBATS

Samhain: 31 October

Yule: 21 December

Imbolg: 2 February

Oestara: 21 March

Beltane: 1 May

Litha: 21 June

Lammas: 1 August

Madron: 21 September

These eight Sabbats are the major festivals in the Witches' year. Taken together, they form the Wheel of the Year. At these festivals Witches celebrate the seasons, the agricultural cycle of sowing, growing and reaping, and the cycle of the Goddess and the God.

If you have read other material on the Craft, you may notice that some of the Sabbat names are familiar but some are different, even if only in spelling. Witchcraft dates from a time when writing was not common and spelling was not regulated. The Sabbats, whilst celebrated in similar ways, would have had different names depending on where the participants lived and what language and even dialect they spoke. The names I have given above are those most often used by my own Covens, but I will give some of the alternatives in the descriptions of the Sabbats themselves. As an individual, or Solitary, Witch, you can use whichever names seem most comfortable to you, although again it is a good idea to stick within one tradition, i.e. don't mix Celtic with Egyptian with Norse. If you are working within a Coven then you will be required to use the names, and themes, that the group uses when doing group workings. If you do additional Solitary work (and many Witches who belong to a Coven do also work on their own, subject to their High Priestess's approval), then you can revert to your favoured titles at these times.

The Sabbats are divided into two groups, the Major and Minor Sabbats:

⭐ Samhain, Imbolg, Beltane and Lammas are Major Sabbats, of which Samhain is the greatest, with Beltane next in importance. The Major Sabbats are the ancient fire festivals, and fire, or more often these days candles, is still used to celebrate them. Samhain and Beltane are both intercalary days, that is days outside the old calendar. On these two days the veil between the worlds of the living and the dead is said to be at its thinnest and this is a traditional time for scrying or divination. In times past people did not have access to calendars and would have celebrated these festivals in tune with seasonal 'clues' – Imbolg when the first buds appeared on the trees, Beltane when the May blossom first appeared, Lammas at the start of the harvest and Samhain with the first frosts. Thus the date of celebration would have varied from place to place depending on the regional climate. In the part of Norfolk where I live, for example, the trees bud a week or two earlier than many more northern parts of England. Some Witches still use the old system of watching for natural signs to date their festivals. However, in today's busy world it is often simpler to plan the festivals by the calendar. Additionally, it is often said that there is a three-day 'window' in which the Sabbats can be celebrated, that is, the Sabbat can be celebrated the day before, the day of or the day after the date given above.

⭐ Yule and Litha are Solstices. At Yule the days are at their shortest and the nights are at their longest. At Litha the days reach their greatest length and the night is at its shortest. Oestara and Madron are the Equinoxes. At these times the length of day and night is equal. Because the cycle of the Earth around the Sun is not exactly the same length as our year, the dates of both the Solstices and Equinoxes are not fixed, and the Solstice or Equinox may actually fall on 20th or 22nd of the month. The Solstices and Equinoxes together are referred to as the Minor Sabbats. Many Witches will consult an astrological almanac and celebrate these festivals on the precise date and in extreme cases at the precise time. However, it is almost certain that traditionally our forebears would have celebrated the event a few days after the actual Sabbat, as they had no accurate clocks, let alone access to almanacs, and would have to have waited until they could have actually seen the changing day length. Again, the majority of Witches will use the three-day window approach towards setting the date of celebration.

You may have noticed that the dates of the Sabbats coincide with the dates of many Christian festivals and those of other religions and, as we shall see later, the content of the celebration is similar, too, especially for Samhain All Souls' Eve, Yule/Christmas, Imbolg/Candlemas, Oestara/Easter and Madron/Harvest Festival. This is not really surprising, as it has long been suspected, and recent evidence confirms, that most religions have their roots either in the Celtic peoples or in the ancient land of Sumer. The Celts and Sumerians worshipped Gods and Goddesses and believed in Magic, balance and many other concepts that Witches hold to be true.

In addition to this it is customary, not to mention logical, when trying to overlay another belief system, to maintain the existing festivals and sites of worship, so that the population can continue to visit the same places at the same times for the same (or similar) reasons. In this way change is less obvious and less likely to cause opposition. This is especially true in the case of older religions which were accustomed to newcomers having Gods and Goddesses of different names and were quite happy to let these be worshipped alongside their own deities.

Beltane used to be celebrated as May Day until Cromwell outlawed it as Pagan (a derogatory term at that time). Strangely enough, this festival has been reinstated fairly recently into our calendar with the May Day Bank Holiday. Litha, the longest day, is the feast of St John the Baptist, one of the most important figures in Christianity outside the Trinity. It is celebrated by many as his feast or more often these days simply as midsummer. I have more than once been invited to join local churches in this celebration of the Summer Solstice! This leaves only Lammas as the 'stranger' to most people and even then there is the first August Bank Holiday to remind us of this traditional festival.

It is often said by modern Witches that the Sabbats are a time for celebration, not a time for Magical working, and this is a valid point of view. Magic, the work of Witches, can be performed at all the phases of the Moon, hence time for reflection on the passage of the year and for celebrating the cycles of the Goddess and the God should be set aside. However, the tides of energy are very strong at the Sabbats and sometimes it can be appropriate to perform Magical working at these times. This is not to say that you must perform Magic at every Sabbat, nor is it a good idea to save your Magical workings for them, as many problems simply cannot be left until the appropriate Sabbat comes around. Also, many can be solved without the added energy of a Sabbat.

So, how do Witches celebrate the Sabbats? The celebration can take many forms, depending on the circumstances of the individual, but for those who are part of a Coven or who have links, however distant, with one, these are times for getting together. Witches will travel many miles to return to a group with which they have strong links, taking days off work, paying for accommodation or sleeping on their High Priestess's floor in order to celebrate together. This is especially true of the Major Sabbats.

Witches who work on their own, whether through choice or necessity, may perform rituals or choose less obvious ways of celebrating the Wheel of the Year. This is especially true for individuals who live with others who may not accept the Craft. I worked as a Solitary for many years and have celebrated the festivals with anything from work done in the garden to silent meditation on a walk through the woods.

In the following pages you will find suggestions for celebrating each of the Sabbats in a variety of ways and once you understand the content and meaning of the festivals you can devise your own ways of marking them meaningfully for yourself. As I have said before, this book is written primarily for people who are new to the Craft and who might not be living in a Witchcraft-friendly environment, so all the rituals for the Sabbats given here should be accessible, however difficult your domestic arrangements. (You will find more detailed information on working ritual and adapting it to suit your lifestyle in Chapter 6, 'Magic', and Chapter 7, 'Spellcraft and Herb Lore'.)

SAMHAIN

31 OCTOBER

Samhaine, All Souls, All Hallows Eve, Halloween

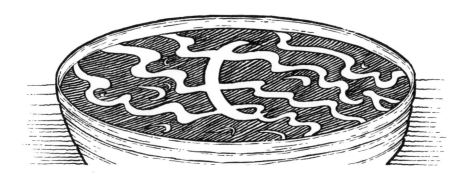

Most usually pronounced 'Sow'ain', this is the most important festival in the Witch's year. Samhain marks the beginning and the end of the Wheel of the Year in the same way that New Year does in the conventional calendar. Samhain starts as soon as it becomes dark on the evening of 31 October and celebrations are often timed to commence, or to peak, at midnight. However, rituals and celebration are often held on 1 November, the first day of the 'New Year', or even on 2 November, if Samhain commitments overrun.

Samhain has a reputation for being linked with death, the spirits of the dead and with all kinds of 'spookiness'. This reputation is in some respects deserved. This festival marks the point in the year when the winter months are definitely on their way. In the past it was a time when people took stock of their supplies for the winter: how much grain they had gathered, how many animals they had. Where supplies were short, they would assess which of the animals were likely to last through the cold months and slaughter those which were unlikely to survive, preserving the meat for later use and saving precious feed for the animals which would make best use of it. In some cultures, such as those living in the Arctic Circle, the elderly of the tribe would refuse to eat at this time, effectively sacrificing themselves for the good of their people. Everywhere there would have been great feasts at Samhain, as this could have been the last opportunity for fresh food until life returned in the spring.

Samhain is also one of the intercalary days of the old Celtic calendar, a day outside the 'normal' year, when the veil between the worlds of the living and the dead is considered to be at its thinnest. For Witches this means that this is a time when it is possible for the spirits of the dead to return to their loved ones and we will set aside a special place at the Samhain feast for any spirits who do care to join us. We do not, however, summon spirits to be with us, as we feel that it is not right to disturb the peace of those who have gone before, unless they are willing. It is traditional at this time to light a candle in the window to guide the welcome spirits home and to deter any unwanted spirits. This is the origin of the Halloween pumpkin lanterns.

Witches also believe that this is when the Wild Hunt begins, when the Horned God rides with his hounds and gathers up the souls of those who linger and those who are unwary. The Wild Hunt continues throughout the winter months. Some Covens will enact the Hunt by setting a challenging course through the woods for the members, or runners as they are sometimes called. Finishing the course whilst keeping to the rules will bring special gifts. Those who fail the Hunt must make an offering to the Lord of the Hunt of a nature appropriate to the setting in which they competed. In our group this usually involves returning to the site in daylight to clear litter, tend the plants or otherwise contribute to that specific environment. However, as it is quite unwise for a Solitary Witch to take off into unknown woods in the middle of the night, there are alternatives. I myself have written a Pathworking which allows the individual to experience the challenge of the Wild Hunt without putting themselves at physical risk. Alternatively, you can set yourself a personal challenge, which you then dedicate to the Hunter. This means you must be very honest with yourself as to whether it is a fair challenge and whether or not you have succeeded. If you do choose to do this, it is a good idea to plan your challenge in advance and aim to complete it on or around Samhain, so that you are in a position to make your offering as soon after the feast as possible.

At this time of year the Goddess takes on her role as Crone or Wise One, so we look to her for wisdom and guidance. This takes the form of many kinds of divination such as the tarot, Dark Mirror or other forms of scrying. In the Coven setting the High Priest may invoke the spirit of the Crone into the High Priestess and, thus inspired, she will speak to the group, either all together or individually.

A SAMHAIN RITUAL

There are three main themes for this Sabbat. The Goddess takes on the role of Wise One, so we practise divination and scrying to seek wisdom. The God leads out the Wild Hunt, so we face challenge and make a personal sacrifice if we fail. It is the end of the old year, the beginning of the new and a time when the veil between the worlds is thin, so we light a candle and set a place at the feast to welcome those we have loved who have gone before.

Set aside some quiet time when you will be undisturbed, after Sunset on 31 October. Have ready a black candle and a white candle, some feasting food and drink. If you wish to do some divination you will need to have ready your tools of divination, whether tarot cards, runes or whatever. If you have undertaken a challenge, you may wish to include some small reminder of it, whether you succeeded or failed.

When you are ready, settle down and call upon each of the four elements of Air, Fire, Water and Earth, asking each to be with you.

Next visualize the Goddess as Crone and the God as Hunter and ask them to join you (see pages 35–36 for more information on this).

Now light the black candle, which represents the passing year, and spend a short while thinking about what has happened in your life and the lives of those around you in the last 12 months. Give thanks to the Lord and Lady for the good things and successes. And consider what you may have learned from the failures and problems. Also remember anyone dear to you, whether human or pet, who has passed from this world in the past year.

Next light the white candle, which represents the New Year, and spend a short while thinking about the things you hope to achieve and see happen, and ask the Lord and Lady to give their blessings on these hopes.

If you wish to perform a divination, this is the time to do so, when both the candles of the old and new are lit. (For more on divination, see pages 27–31.) Make sure you have a pencil and paper to hand to record any thoughts you have and images you receive.

If you have undertaken a challenge, give thanks to the Lord and Lady for your success or state what your offering to the Lord of the Hunt will be.

Now you can put out the black candle and say a final farewell to the old year.

Next you perform the Rite of Wine and Cakes (see pages 143–144).

Thank the elements individually, in the same sequence in which you invited them, for their presence. Then thank the Lord and Lady for their guidance.

Your ritual is over and all that remains is to enjoy your feast. As this is Samhain, it is traditional to set a place for the spirits of your loved ones at the feast. When working alone, simply put aside a small portion of whatever you have to eat and put this outside in the garden when you next go out, or on the window ledge.

When all is done, tidy away after yourself. Try not to think of this as a chore, but rather as part of the ritual. I usually find that this is the time to think about the significance of what has taken place. If you are able, let the white candle burn a while longer, but under no circumstances should you leave it unattended.

OTHER WAYS OF MARKING SAMHAIN

✸ Wait until the first very cold or even frosty day which marks this season (if you are in the Southern Hemisphere then you will need some other seasonal marker) and go for a walk. Look at nature and reflect upon the changes you see, the signs of life as well as the signs that a period of the year is over. Think about the way these changes are reflected in your own life. In doing so you will find yourself closer to the natural cycle of life, death and rebirth. Remember that in nature, death and decay are just a natural resting point before new life and new growth.

✸ As this is a festival of the dead, it is a good time to remember those who have gone before, not in a melancholy way but by laying particular emphasis on the things you shared and the achievements of that person. There are many ways to do this – look through old photographs and remember the good times, make a visit to someone's burial site or to a location you shared together, read their favourite book or poem, or listen to a piece of music you enjoyed together. All are good ways of celebrating the life of someone you have loved. For that matter you could always use these things to focus on and remember absent or distant friends, as well as taking the more practical step of finding their address and writing a letter.

✸ Take up a new form of divination or work on one you have already started. Often we neglect these skills, so that when we really want to use them we are unsure of them. Be sure to keep a record of your study and your results, as this will help you to develop your ability. The following technique assumes that you have decided to learn the tarot, but the method can easily be adapted to many other forms of divination.

✧ Take a tarot deck, preferably a fully pictorial one, i.e. one that has illustrations on the cards of both the Major and Minor Arcarnas, as opposed to one which shows seven swords for the Seven of Swords. Put the booklet that came with them back into the box unread. This is important, for if you are to master a form of divination it is your interpretation which matters, not the one written by someone else.

✧ Shuffle the cards. If you are doing the reading in the morning, think about the day ahead; if in the evening, think about the next day.

✧ Select the top three cards, nominating one for the morning, one for the afternoon and one for the evening.

✧ Look carefully at each card in turn, examining the picture carefully to see whether you can 'see' the story in the card. It can help to ask yourself what is happening in the picture, what has happened and what might happen next.

✧ Note down the cards, your thoughts and interpretation (if any).

✧ Once you have done this for all three cards, put them away and forget about them.

✧ The next day, refer back to your three cards and your notes. Compare what happened in your day with your notes and with the cards themselves. Look for similarities and links.

✧ If you do this two or three times a week you will soon find that you have mastered the tarot without the need for constant reference or the need to spend hours memorizing a list of meanings.

YULE

21 DECEMBER

The Winter Solstice, Christmas

The Winter Solstice is the shortest day and the longest night. Because it is an astronomical event, the actual date will vary from year to year, but, as mentioned earlier, many Witches will celebrate it on 21 December anyway.

The Sabbat of Yule is the festival of the rebirth of the Sun. Having been in decline since the Summer Solstice, the Sun now begins to increase in strength, so that even in the depths of winter we are reminded that life will begin again. Witches will bring evergreen decorations into the home as a reminder of the return of the growing season and this is the origin of the Christmas tree and decorations. Holly with berries is a favourite, the red of the berries symbolizing the resting Mother and the life returning to the land, and the dark green Holly symbolizing the Holly King, who rules until this time. Mistletoe is another decoration with strong Pagan connections. The plant has long been considered Magical because it grows between the earth and the sky, and is not rooted in the ground.

Many people, not just Witches, will go out just before dawn on the Winter Solstice so that they can watch the Sun rise and welcome the returning Sun King. This is not as bad as it sounds, because at this time of year the Sun rises relatively late and there is usually some light for at least an hour before the Sun appears above the horizon.

At Yule, the Oak King, Lord of Summer, is reborn. In legend the Oak and Holly Kings are brothers who share the rule of the year, with the Oak King reigning from midwinter to midsummer, the period of increasing light, and the Holly King reigning from midsummer to midwinter, the period of increasing darkness. In this way they represent light and dark individually, and balance when viewed over the whole year. Light and dark are not used as euphemisms for good and bad here, for we need both halves of the year to prosper.

At the Solstices, light and dark are said to battle to determine which will have control over the coming months and many Covens will re-enact the fight between the Oak and Holly Kings, making sure, of course, that the 'right' King wins.

The Wild Hunt which started at Samhain is now at its height and it is said that anyone who is unwary enough to be out at midnight on the Winter Solstice will be swept up by the Hunter and carried away.

To mark this Sabbat many people will prepare a Yule Log. The traditional Yule Log is not the chocolate-covered Swiss roll variety, but a real log onto which will be placed a number of candles. To make this safe it is necessary to have a log which sits firmly and doesn't roll, scattering hot wax and fire in all directions! Each person in the group, Coven or family will light one candle, representing the return of the days of increasing light, and will express a wish for the forthcoming season. Traditionally the Yule Log would then be retained until the following year, when it would be placed in the hearth and allowed to burn. However, these days very few people have an open fire in which to burn their log, so it is often simply retained for use the following year. Having said that, some groups will use a chocolate log in the same way, with one small candle for each member of the celebration. After the candles have been lit and the wishes stated, the log is eaten.

A YULE RITUAL

The main themes of this festival are the rebirth of the Sun, the start of the days of increasing light and the rise of the Oak King.

The simplest way to celebrate Yule is to rise before dawn to greet the rising Sun. Many diaries and almanacs will give the time of the rising and setting of the Sun, and for that matter, the Moon. If you live near the sea, tide-tables will perform the same function. If it is possible, go out, preferably to a high place, to watch the Sun rise. Alternatively, choose a window facing the direction of Sunrise. As before, call upon the elements, the Goddess and the God to be with you. As the Sun rises above the horizon, give thanks for the return of the light and warmth that it brings.

This is the very beginning of the return of new life to the land, the spark of light which brings promise with it. As a time of beginnings it is also a time to reflect upon any new starts you may wish to make and perhaps dedicate them to the returning Sun. If you are outside, look around you for a stone, pebble or twig – you are sure to see something which catches your eye – and take this as a reminder of the promise you have decided to make.

OTHER WAYS OF MARKING YULE

✷ Bring foliage into the house, either holly or any other seasonal plant(s). You easily can incorporate these into the household's festive decorations.

✷ Prepare an edible Yule Log. You can purchase ready-made ones, but as intent is all-important in Witchcraft, it is better to make your own, and frankly they usually taste better. Decorate it with melted chocolate and powdered icing sugar (to represent the frosts of this season). Place one candle on it for everyone who will be present when it is to be used. The kind with their own holders sold for birthday cakes work very well. If you wish you can also place a robin on it. The robin is one of many birds with very strong Pagan connotations, not least because it is usually more obvious at this time of year.

✷ Light a Yule candle, which should be gold or a golden orange in colour. Prepare it by dedicating it to the rising Sun and the days of increasing light. This is done by stroking the candle from the centre to the ends whilst visualizing the rise of the Sun. Ideally, the candle should be lit before Sunrise on the first day of increasing light and should be allowed to burn out. However, in practical terms you never leave a burning candle unattended, so you can light the candle for a few minutes then put it out. Relight it every day after the Solstice, remembering the reasons why we celebrate this festival, until it is all gone.

✷ One other way of celebrating this and every Sabbat is to look at the legends of Gods and Goddesses which are associated with the festival. You do not need to spend a lot of money on books to do this. Most libraries will have books on Greek and Roman mythology, and by using the bibliographies in such books you can track down others of interest.

ule you are looking for legends of Solar deities who repeat the theme of the rising and reborn God, e.g. Mithras, Dionysus and Adonis. You might also like to look at the legend of the Oak and Holly King or the legends associated with the robin. Don't just read them as amusing folk tales, think about the lessons and truths they contain, for there was a time when all knowledge was handed down in story or song, and these are all that remain to us of the ancient wisdom.

IMBOLG

2 FEBRUARY

Imbolc, Oimelc, Festival of Bride (pronounced 'Breed'), Festival of Bridgit, Candlemas

At Imbolg the spark of light born at Yule becomes a flame to warm the people and the land. Now we see the first signs of spring. The trees are in bud and some flowers (snowdrops for example) begin to blossom. The word 'Imbolg'

means 'in the belly', whilst 'Oimelc' means 'ewe's milk'. Both refer to the fact that many ewes are pregnant at this time and in a mild year the first lambs will be born about now. Imbolg is the quickening of the year, the time when the Earth is made pregnant with the promise of summer fruitfulness and the harvest to come.

At Imbolg the Goddess casts aside the robes of Wise One and returns as Maiden, dressed in white. In some groups a Maiden will be chosen and will wear a crown of lights and a white robe or cloak for the ritual. It is worth noting that up until relatively recently, the term 'maiden' was used to denote a female who had not yet given birth to child, so that even an obviously pregnant married woman could be a maiden and take this role in ritual. The God, who was reborn at Yule, is now seen as a young man, full of vigour, and his pursuit of the Maiden starts at this Sabbat.

Imbolg is the time when the last of Yule's festive evergreens are removed. In some places it is still traditional to hold on to the (undecorated) Christmas fir until Imbolg, when it is taken and burned on the Imbolg fires. These days few of us can afford to keep the tree in place, especially as our modern forced and treated trees find it hard to keep their needles until January, let alone a whole month later. However, there is a practical alternative. As part of my Imbolg celebrations I take all the Yule and Christmas cards I have been given and recycle them, either making them into gift tags for the following year or cutting out the pictures to give to a local playgroup.

In ancient Rome this was a festival of Pan and the priests of Pan, called the Luperci, would run through the streets dressed in goatskin cloth whipping the people, especially women, to make them fertile for the coming year.

In many parts of the British Isles you will find wells dedicated to Bride or to the Christian St Bridget. Originally these would have been associated with the Goddess. If you are lucky enough to live near one of these, or able to visit one, look for a nearby tree with scraps of fabric tied to its branches. This will be a 'wishing tree'. Many people, whether Witches, Pagans or otherwise, visit these places to make an offering to the Goddess in the hope of having a wish granted. Such offerings are usually a strip of cloth, but I have seen necklaces of plaited grasses, small posies of flowers and even a child's shoe tied to a wishing tree. If you do visit such a site and wish to leave an offering, try to make it something which will soon return to the Earth – a small circlet of grass plaited whilst thinking about your wish, or a hair from your own head, offered as a form of sacrifice. Look in your local press for notices of well-dressing celebrations, as many of these still take place at this time of year.

AN IMBOLG RITUAL

This festival is the first rite of spring. The dark of winter is behind us and now the Goddess takes on the robes of the Maiden and the God is seen as a young man.

Find some time and a place where you will be undisturbed. Take a black or dark red candle to represent the Goddess as Wise One and a white one to represent her as Maiden. As with all your rituals, call upon the elements of Air, Fire, Water and Earth as well as the Goddess and the God to be with you.

Light the dark candle and say, 'This light is the light of the Crone, the Wise One who has ruled over the winter months, the resting time.' Spend a few moments thinking of all that has passed since your celebration of Samhain, especially of what you have learned in this time.

Next say, 'Now it is time for the Crone to turn away and become once more the Maiden, Lady of Spring and of promise.' Light the white candle and extinguish the dark one.

Now spend a little time thinking about what you would like to begin in this new season.

Thank the elements and the Goddess and the God for their presence during your rites.

An alternative to this ritual would be to take some ice, a large piece if possible, and, taking it in your strong hand (your right if right handed, your left if left handed), hold it over a bowl and say, 'This represents the Crone, Lady of Winter, of the time when the land is still and resting. But as winter's thaw begins, so the Lady casts off her robes of stillness and becomes once more the Maiden. Full of movement, like the cool waters of spring, she flows once more to bring life and hope to all the land.'

Once the ice has fully melted, keep the resulting water to put on your favourite plant, either indoors or in the garden. Please wait until the water has reached a reasonable temperature before you do this, otherwise you will freeze the poor thing's roots!

Once again, this ritual should begin by asking the support of the elements, the Goddess and the God, and they should be thanked at the end.

OTHER WAYS OF MARKING IMBOLG

★ As this is a time of new life and growth, it is appropriate to plant bulbs or flowers or to sow seeds. However, you will need to use your judgement and some local knowledge to decide whether to actually do so at Imbolg or whether to wait a week (or several) until the last frosts have passed. Of course seeds can often be started indoors and planted out a month or so later.

A word of caution here – if you are unlucky and your seedlings or plants fail, try not to read anything 'significant' into this. Unless and until you are an experienced and seasoned gardener, or unless you naturally have 'green fingers', you are quite likely to have a less than impressive success rate the first few times.

If you don't have access to a garden, you can always choose an indoor plant to nurture. Many of the herbs that Witches use in their Magic, as well as their kitchen, will grow quite happily on a window sill. Rosemary and lavender are perhaps the two most useful, as well as having a pleasant scent all year round.

⭐ If you are lucky enough to live near a suitable tree, choose one to be 'your own'. This is the tree that you will watch to mark the seasons. Observe its cycles of growth and fruitfulness, the way it reacts to the seasons. By doing this you will have a natural link to the Wheel of the Year. It is better to choose a tree which does shed its leaves in winter rather than an evergreen, as the cycles of the latter can be very difficult to see. There are many trees which have particular significance to Witches; oak, ash, hawthorn, elder, willow, rowan and many others. If your tree is in your own garden or in an accessible place, then you will be able to visit it and even meditate under it whenever you please. You may even find that this is the tree which gives you the wood for your wand.

⭐ Read and learn about trees, especially those native to your land and those considered significant to the Craft.

OESTARA

21 MARCH

Oestre, Eostar, the Spring Equinox

It is no coincidence that the name for this Sabbat sounds similar to the word 'Easter'. Eostre, or Ostara, is an Anglo-Saxon Dawn Goddess whose symbols are the egg and the hare. She, in turn, is the European version of the Goddess Ishtar or Astarte, whose worship dates back thousands of years and is certainly pre-Christian. Eostre also lives on in our medical language in the words 'oestrous' (the sexual impulse in female animals) and 'oestrogen' (a female hormone). Today, Oestara is celebrated as a spring festival. Although the Goddess put on the robes of Maiden at Imbolg, here she is seen as truly embodying the spirit of spring. By this time we can see all around us the awakened land, the leaves on the trees, the flowers and the first shoots of corn.

Oestara is also the Spring Equinox, a time of balance when day and night are equal. As with the other Equinox and the Solstices, the date of this festival may move slightly from year to year, but many will choose to celebrate it on 21 March. In keeping with the balance of the Equinox, Oestara is a time when we seek balance within ourselves. It is a time for throwing out the old and taking on the new. We rid ourselves of those things which are no longer necessary – old habits, thoughts and feelings – and take on new ideas and thoughts. This does not mean that you use this festival as a time for berating yourself about your 'bad' points, but rather that you should seek to find a balance through which you can accept yourself for what you are.

There is some debate as to whether Oestara or Imbolg was the traditional time of spring cleaning, but certainly the casting out of the old would seem to be in sympathy with the spirit of this festival and the increased daylight at this time encourages a good clean out around the home.

AN OESTARA RITUAL

The main points of this Sabbat are those of balance and of spring.

This ritual is best performed outdoors. In advance you will need to collect a small handful of old leaves and write on each something that you would like to be rid of. Also take a small number of seeds or seedlings (if these seedlings come from the seeds you planted at Imbolg, so much the better), one for each new thing that you wish to attain.

Silently ask the elements, the Goddess and the God to be with you, then when you are ready, dig a hole large enough to give space to the seedlings you wish to grow and place the dead leaves into it. Say, 'Lord and Lady of this time of balance, these are the things I wish to be rid of. As these leaves wither and rot, may I let go of those things that might hold me back.'

Next place one or two seedlings on top of the leaves. Say, 'Lord and Lady, these are the things which I wish to attain in the coming season. Let them grow strong and true from the remains of the old.'
As before, thank the elements, the Goddess and the God.

Remember that for ritual to work, you should give more thought to your preparations than the time you actually spend performing the ritual. In this case, that preparation includes carefully choosing the things you wish to leave behind and the things you wish to take on. On a more practical level, it will also include selecting plants appropriate to your area and climate, as well as a suitable place to plant them. If you cannot perform your ritual outside, then you can either scale down everything and work with a single plant pot or you can dedicate your leaves and plant indoors and go out to plant them at a later date.

OTHER WAYS OF MARKING OESTARA

✴ Celebrate the arrival of spring with flowers. Bring them into your own home and, in keeping with the theme of balance, give them to others. You do not have to spend a lot of money – one or two blooms given for no other reason than 'spring is here' can often bring a smile to even the most gloomy face.

✴ Do a bit of 'personal housekeeping'. We live in an age where guilt is more often encouraged than pride, where we are encouraged to dwell upon our 'negative' points and habits. This is not the way of the Witch. As Witches we must learn to be as honest about our plus points as society would like us to be about our minuses.

Advertising, probably the most pervasive kind of propaganda, encourages us to think of ourselves as 'less than perfect' unless we look and dress like the people in the adverts and possess all the things that the advertisers would like us to spend money on. It is worth bearing in mind that if we truly needed these products then there would be no need to put them into commercials!

However, to return to the 'personal housekeeping', write a list of 20 of your plus points, things you are good at, and 20 minus points, things you would like to improve. Try not to be influenced by stereotypes – many female Witches include 'outspoken' on their list of negatives, while males will describe the same quality as positive! If you absolutely must include your physical attributes on the minus list, then make sure that these are things which you can sensibly expect to change, but don't fall into the advertisers' trap. From the perspective of the Witch it is far more important that you should come to terms with the person you are, rather than worry about the way you look, as it is who you are which will ultimately determine the way people see you. In my own case I am a fairly average-looking slightly overweight person of average height, but many see me as quite tall, slender and even imposing!

One of the first tasks of the Witch is to understand and accept themselves, with all their good and bad points, because it is only when you understand yourself that you will be in a position to understand others, and therein lies a good portion of Witches' Magic.

★ Start to learn about some of the plants and herbs which have been traditionally used as remedies. A basic knowledge of herbs is part of the heritage of the Witch. You will find a small selection in Chapter 7, 'Spellcraft and Herb Lore'. Consider growing some of these yourself. Read a good herbal or find a herbalist who can teach you more.

BELTANE

1 MAY

Beltan, Bealtaine, Walpurgisnacht, May Day

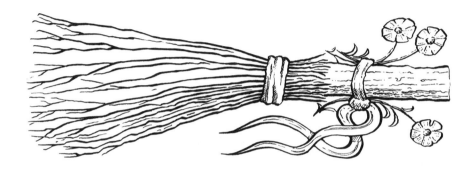

Beltane is the second most important Sabbat in the Witches' calendar after Samhain. Again, it is an intercalary day when the veil between the worlds of the living and the dead is thin. But whereas Samhain is a time for greeting and celebrating those who have gone before, Beltane is a time when more mischievous spirits may take advantage. For this reason the results of divinations performed at Beltane should always be approached cautiously, for the Gods also enjoy a sense of humour! Similarly, be very careful of working Magic at this time, for the phrase 'Be careful what you wish for' is even more appropriate around Beltane. Many a Witch has found a wish being granted very literally and has received what they asked for as opposed to what they wanted.

This is the festival of the fire God Bel. Bel has been worshipped under many names in all parts of the world for thousands of years: Bel, Beli, Balar,

Balor, Belenus, Baal and Belial. Traditionally, Beltane would be the night on which the old hearth fires were extinguished and the new were kindled from the Bel fire. These fires were placed on the top of hills and produced a chain of beacons which ran across the land. Cattle would be driven between the fires and people would leap over them to ensure fertility for the coming season. In Britain, the tradition of hilltop fires has seen something of a revival lately, although not necessarily associated with Beltane. Fire beacons were lit at the passing of Princess Diana and to mark the Millennium celebrations.

Now the Goddess takes on her robes of Mother, the God descends to reign beside his Queen and the marriage of the Goddess and the God is celebrated. It is said that throughout the spring the God has pursued his mate until at Beltane she allows him to catch her! You can see remnants of this tale in the choosing of a May Queen to rule over May Day. Traditionally, she would then select her consort for the day, although this part of the festivities is often neglected now.

Because of the marriage of the Goddess and the God, this Sabbat is also a major fertility festival. In times past, the Maypole would be central to the Beltane celebrations – a tall pole surmounted by a circlet of flowers which would descend as the ribbons were wound tight by the dancers. This symbol of sexual union would be hard to mistake. Those who had not yet found a partner would seek one at the Beltane rites, wearing green to announce their intentions. They would then spend the night in the woods consummating their new-found love. This is in part the reason why it is considered unlucky to bring the flower of the May tree into the house at this time – after all, if you spent your night in the woods gathering flowers, you had obviously been unlucky in your search for a mate! No wonder, then, that the Puritans abolished the holiday in an attempt to stop the celebrating of Beltane!

Beltane is a common time for Witches to Handfast. A Handfasting is the Wiccan form of wedding. Unlike its Christian counterpart, both parties approach the ceremony as equals (neither is 'given away'), they write their own vows and make their promises directly to each other, not through an intermediary, although a Priestess and/or Priest may assist them in the ceremony. Many of the phrases and traditions used for weddings of all denominations have their roots in this older form of union. 'Tying the knot' and 'getting hitched' are references to the part of a Handfasting where the couple's hands are literally tied together with a gold and silver cord whilst they make their promises. 'Jumping the broom' (a phrase less well known today than 30 years ago) refers to the point at which the couple join hands and leap over the broomstick (which itself is a symbol of the union of male and female) to signify their leap from one life (that of being single) to another (that of being married). Handfasting need not be for life; there are in fact three periods of time for which your vows may stand: a year and a day, a life-time and for all time. Obviously both parties must be in agreement as to the term of their joining.

Central to the celebration of Beltane is the Great Rite. Most often cele-brated symbolically, this is the ritual form of the union between the Goddess and the God. The Goddess is represented by the Chalice or Cup full of wine and the God is represented by the Athame (the Witches' knife). In full ritual within a Coven, or partnership, the Goddess is invoked into the High Priestess and the God is invoked into the High Priest. The High Priest will hold the Chalice high in front of the group, telling them to behold the symbol of the Goddess. He will then kneel in front of the High Priestess, who will hold the Athame and likewise tell them to behold the symbol of the God. Then she will lower the blade of the Athame into the wine, whilst both will speak of the joining of Goddess and God from which all life flows. The Great Rite actual is generally reserved for ritual between partners or for cer-tain kinds of initiation, where it may in fact be performed in token rather than in full.

At first it appears from this that you cannot celebrate the Great Rite alone, but this is not so. The words of the invocation make it clear that the

Chalice and Athame themselves represent the Goddess and the God, so that their union can be celebrated by any Witch, whether in company or when working Solitary.

The following form of the Great Rite is one suitable for a Witch working on their own. It has been shortened and slightly simplified from the more formal Great Rite as conducted by a Coven. However, as with all ritual and Magic, if your intent is true, then your simple rite will be just as powerful as a more complex form.

A BELTANE RITUAL

The main themes of this Sabbat are the fire festival of Bel and its associated fertility rites. The Goddess takes on her role of Mother, the God descends to rule beside his Queen and so the celebration of this union of fertility takes place through the Great Rite.

By far the most obvious way of celebrating Beltane in a traditional way is to perform the Great Rite. For this you will need a Chalice of wine and an Athame (see page 136 to find ritual substitutions). As in preceding rituals, you will need to find a time and a place where you will be undisturbed.

Ask for the support of the elements and then visualize the Goddess in her robes of Mother, warm and caring, strong and full of grace, and ask her to be present at your rite. Visualize the God as a young man full of strength and energy and ask him also to be with you.

Take your Chalice and hold it in both hands in front of you at eye level. Focus on the image of the Goddess and say, 'Behold the Chalice,

symbol of the Goddess, the Great Mother who brings fruitfulness and knowledge to all.'

Put the Chalice down and take your Athame. Hold this in both hands in front of you, blade pointing upwards, also at eye level, and, focusing on the image of the God, say, 'Behold the Athame, symbol of the God, the All Father who brings energy and strength to all.'

Then change the position of your Athame so that you are holding it blade downwards in your right, or strong, hand, take the Chalice in the other hand and, lowering the blade into the wine, say, 'Joined in union together, they bring life to all.'

Kiss the handle of your Athame, say, 'Blessed Be,' and then put it down.

Next take a sip of your wine whilst meditating on the roles of the Goddess and the God at this time of year.

After you have finished, remember to thank the elements and the Goddess and the God. Any remaining wine can be drunk as part of your feasting or, if you prefer, you may take it outside and pour it on the ground as a libation.

OTHER WAYS OF MARKING BELTANE

✴ If you are fortunate, you may well find a May Day celebration taking place near you, perhaps Maypole dancing, Morris dancing or a May fair, in which case it is worth attending, for however watered down our old traditions might be, they still contain the seeds of the old ways. Beltane was always a time when the whole community would join together to celebrate the onset of summer and being with others reminds us of the continuity of our beliefs.

✹ Flowers, berries and foliage form a major part of the decorations for every Sabbat. At this time of year it is traditional for the young to wear chaplets (circular crowns) of flowers. You may not feel inclined to go out wearing one, but it evokes the sentiments of the season to make one as an indoor decoration. As you do not have to fit it to your head, it can be of any size, and if you don't feel confident enough to start from scratch, most florists sell circles woven from wood or cane for a reasonable cost and you can reuse these at every Sabbat if you wish. Decorate your chaplet with white for the departing Maiden, red for the ascending Mother and a good strong bright green for the God as a youth.

✹ This is an excellent time to look at the legends surrounding the Gods and Goddesses known for their sense of humour: Baubo, Sheila na Gig and especially the 'trickster' Gods Loki, Pan and Puck.

✹ Alternatively, you could spend some time looking at colour correspondences and the uses to which colour can be put. Colour correspondences are perhaps the most common way to enhance Magical working and this is an excellent time to observe and study them as they are appearing in nature around now.

LITHA

21 JUNE

The Summer Solstice

The Summer Solstice is the longest day and shortest night of the year. From this point onwards the hours of daylight decline. As with the other Solstice and Equinoxes, celebrations may take place on the actual day of the Solstice or just after it.

At this time the reigns of Oak and Holly Kings are reversed and Lord Holly once more comes into his own. The Holly King presides over the waning part of the year and thus is considered the darker of the two. Remember, though, that in Witchcraft light and dark are not terms used to denote good and evil, but are very literal references to the length of day.

Now groups will re-enact the battle of the Oak and Holly Kings, ensuring that this time the Holly King wins. As this is midsummer, we often incorporate this event into a more open celebration, with very little of the Craft being mentioned. We invite friends and family to an outdoor picnic or barbecue, get our 'kings' to dress the part and get the audience to take sides, cheering on their chosen warrior. We then allow the youngest member present to award the winner with a crown. With a little planning this can become an event that everyone can enjoy, regardless of their path. One note of caution: it is important that your warriors practise their battle. On the one hand they need to make it exciting for the audience and the addition of taunts and insults (suitable for the audience to hear, of course!) goes a long way towards making the whole affair far more interesting. More importantly, though, they need to make sure neither of them is going to really injure the other. It is one thing to put on a good display, it is another to end up with the combatants in hospital!

The Goddess at this time of year is still wearing her robes of Mother and she is full of the promise of harvest. It is important to recognize that whilst the God is celebrated through the cycles of life, death and rebirth, the Goddess is the one who presides over these changes. Whilst he will change his persona, she simply changes her aspect.

The Summer Solstice, whilst a cause for celebration, is also a time for a little reflection, for whilst the Sun is at the peak of his power for the year, he is also starting his decline. Of course, while this is true of one hemisphere, for the other the opposite is true, and our midsummer is midwinter for others. In this we are reminded that the cycle of life continues and is never-ending, and that whilst good things grow old and fade away, they give way to new things which have their own place in the world. The cycle of the seasons is like the tides – as one peaks, it prepares to ebb and give way for another to take its place.

Many groups will choose to rise at dawn on the Summer Solstice to greet the Sun on its day of greatest power. This is not confined to Witches or even to Pagan groups – I have twice been asked by Church groups to join them for this, although I don't think that they really considered the older significance of marking the Solstice in this way.

A LITHA RITUAL

The key themes of this Sabbat are the peak of the Sun's power and the start of its decline, the changeover from Holly King to Oak King and the Goddess as Mother, pregnant with the harvest to come and presiding over the changes of the seasons.

In advance, take a clear crystal with a hole in it. Quartz is best but lead crystal or cut glass of the kind found in inexpensive jewellery is just as good. Do shop around for your crystal. It does not have to be expensive – you may well find what you want in a second-hand store. Thread it onto a length, around a half metre, of strong thread, and secure it with a firm knot. Cleanse your crystal, first of all physically by washing it in warm (not hot) soapy water. (Keep the plug in – you don't want it disappearing down the drain!) Then cleanse it psychically, as stones of all kinds can pick up residual energies from everyone who handles them. Do this by holding it under running water for five minutes whilst visualizing all imperfections being washed away.

When you are ready, call upon the elements, the Goddess and the God to support you, as in the previous rituals. Take your crystal and hold it in the light of the Sun. Do not worry if the day is cloudy, the Sun is just as present. Visualize the Sun's rays filling the crystal with light and energy. When you feel that your crystal has been 'charged' in this way, hang it in the window, preferably where it will be sure to catch the Sun's rays. Lastly, thank the elements, the Goddess and the God for their aid.

At any time when you feel particularly in need of the energy of the Sun, you can take your crystal down and carry it with you, or wear it on a cord around your neck. In terms of planetary influences (the Sun is perceived as a planetary body in terms of Magic), the Sun is the source of energy and symbolic of strength, protection, honour and power.

OTHER WAYS OF MARKING LITHA

☆ Try to find some way of being outside for this Sabbat, or at least a part of it. You may be able to rise at dawn to greet the Sun, but if not, take a walk during a part of the day and use this time to observe the cycle of growth and decline. Many plants have already given of their best for the year and will be dying back to make room for others. Reflect on the things in your own life which have run their course and which should now be replaced by new growth. In other plants you will see that the first blooms have gone but that there is a second flowering and this reflects the need we all have from time to time to start old projects anew or to attack old tasks with renewed energy.

☆ Hold a midsummer party. Give it themes of yellow and gold for the Sun's peak and dark and light green for the battle of the Oak and Holly Lords. It may be possible for you have a mock battle in honour of the Oak and Holly Kings, but if you can't, don't let this spoil your enjoyment of the party or the festival.

☆ You might like to visit one of the ancient sacred sites such as a stone circle or similar and reflect upon the peoples who built some of these places as a way of marking the passage of the year and who used them in their own celebration of the Wheel of the Year. If you are fortunate, you may even

be able to purchase a ticket to one of the celebrations which now take place at many of the stone circles, including, once again, Stonehenge, which was closed to such rites for so many years.

☆ Learn about the properties, powers and uses of crystals and gemstones. If you worked on colour correspondences at the last Sabbat you will be able to see where these two specializations complement each other and how you can use them to enhance your knowledge of the elements.

LAMMAS

1 AUGUST

Lughnasadh, Loaf-Mass

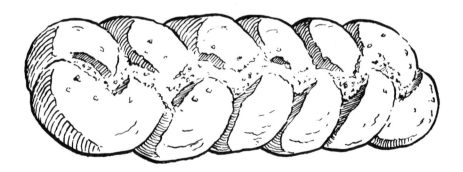

Lammas is the festival of the dying and rising God. Its other name of Lughnasadh (usually pronounced 'Loo-nass-uh' or 'Loo-nass-ar') commemorates the death and subsequent resurrection of the Celtic Sun God Lugh.

Lammas is celebrated at the first of the harvest and it is a festival strongly linked to stories of sacrifice as well as death. Whilst it is almost certain that some ancient traditions did involve blood sacrifice, there are many cases where misunderstanding or misinterpretation of what actually took place gave rise to this idea. It is often said that for people in earlier centuries 'life was cheap'. However, it is a mistake to assume that this meant that the death of a family member or neighbour had any less meaning for the ordinary person than it does now. Communities were much more closely knit in those days and a death would be keenly felt, especially when you consider that everyone had a role to play in the continuance of the group and that there were neither state benefits nor life insurance. Life was only cheap to some of the ruling classes, who considered that those who lived on their land were of no more importance than the cattle they raised alongside them.

It used to be common, and still takes place in one or two isolated areas, for the last sheaf of the first field cut to be 'sacrificed' to the land as a repayment for the bounty of the harvest and to ensure the fertility of the land in coming years. This sacrifice or repayment had to be made quickly, before the spirit of the land awoke and discovered what was happening. The custom was for the whole of the village to gather in the field selected to be the first crop reaped. They would then harvest this as fast as possible and in the ensuing mayhem many small animals and even birds would be caught and killed by the harvesters. Thus, when the true sacrifice of harvested crop was made, the blood in the field would give rise to stories of animals or even people being slaughtered.

Another potentially misleading custom was that of selecting a King for the day. This person would be honoured and for the full day could have anything he wanted, his commands were law. In some tales he is dressed in finery and even wears a crown, in others he may be dressed as the Hobby Horse or

Teaser, or even as a rather grotesque caricature of a giant woman (probably a disguise for the Mother Goddess). During the celebrations he wields a 'sceptre' or stick, with which he strikes people to bring about fertility. Finally at either the start of Sunset or at dawn the following day (both versions appear, as indeed do many variations), he leads the townsfolk to the fields, where everyone gathers around him cheering, laughing, shouting and fooling around before commencing the first harvest. This would take place in much the same way as mentioned above, the King removing his finery, casting it aside and joining with the others to speed the harvesting. To an outside observer, at a time when most people only had one set of clothes and were therefore known by them, it would indeed look as though the King had been slain. Prior to the harvest there was a very prominent person leading everyone; afterwards he was nowhere to be seen and only his clothes remained!

Elements of these harvest rituals can be seen today, although often they are so far removed in time and circumstance from the harvest as to be almost unrecognizable. However, you might like to look carefully at some of the figures you see in carnivals, processions and even at the funfair.

In a variation of the above custom, the first sheaf of corn would be made into a Corn King, a life-size, or almost life-size, image of a man. During the celebrations after the first field had been cleared, this would be slain by all the participants. Many Covens actually make their own Corn King for Lammas which is then 'slaughtered' as part of the ritual. Personally I would advise anyone thinking of doing this to make sure they are doing so outside. The 'slaughter', and to a lesser extent the making, of a Corn King produces a lot of sharp prickly bits of corn which travel all around your home, even getting into the bed, and the last time we did it, I was still finding bits of Corn King all around the house the following Yule!

Some of the remaining corn from that first harvest would be immediately ground into flour to go into the food prepared for the feast, thereby sharing the blessing of the land with the people. In recognition of the Corn King's sacrifice small cakes would be made in the shape of men. This is the origin of our gingerbread men. In ritual a gingerbread man makes a very good substitute for a Corn King, as the remains of your sacrifice do not need to be carefully swept up but can be eaten and enjoyed. Bread for the feast would also be shaped as a man or, more often, as a sheaf of wheat, and from this comes the term Loaf-Mass, another name for this festival.

A LAMMAS RITUAL

The main themes of Lammas are the death and rebirth of the God, the festival of Lugh the Sun God, the first harvest and personal sacrifice to repay what we have been given.

Whereas other Sabbats are sometimes about giving up the old to take on the new, Lammas is concerned with making sure we have given enough for what we have received. Living in a very commercial society it is often easier to think about the things we want but do not have than it is to remember what we already have. Hence Lammas is a good time to consider the positives in life, to count your blessings so to speak. As this is something we are not accustomed to doing, it is a good idea to start your preparation a few days before you intend to celebrate the Sabbat.

Take a number of pieces of paper and on one side make a note of something you have achieved in the past year, or even since your last Sabbat. On the reverse make a note of something you intend to do in 'payment' for this. This should be something you can achieve but which will cost you either time or effort in some way. To give an example, if you have had success in an examination, put that on the first side. On the reverse

you may like to dedicate some time to helping teach someone else a skill they do not have or to reading to a young child. The 'achievement' and 'payment' do not have to be directly linked. You might choose to cook a special meal for someone who deserves it, for example, as payment for your pet's recovery from an illness. Once you start on an exercise like this it can be easy to think of a huge number of positives which have happened in your life. If this is the case, try to restrict yourself to the ones where you feel that you have received the help of the Goddess and aim to mark three key events in this way.

At the time you have set aside for your ritual, call upon the elements, the Goddess and the God in the usual way. Take your first piece of paper and read carefully the 'achievement' whilst remembering the way you felt at the time. Give thanks to the Lord and Lady for giving this to you.

Then turn it over and read your 'payment'. Dedicate this task to the Lord and Lady, saying that you will be doing it in their honour and as payment.

Repeat this with all three.

Once you have finished, thank the elements, the Goddess and the God.

You can either pin your promises up in a place where you can see them, only removing them when you have carried out your tasks, or you can put your papers away in a safe place. Either way, do not forget to carry out your promises, as these have been made and dedicated as a Witch and just as you do not wish the Goddess and the God to stop helping you, so you do not want to fail to carry out your offering to them.

OTHER WAYS OF MARKING LAMMAS

✱ If you prefer to mark the festival of the dying and rising God in a more direct manner and you have a God symbol in your home, you might like to cover this with a black cloth for the day before the Sabbat and uncover it as a part of your ritual, or even as a separate rite. To honour the newly risen God it is appropriate to bring a gold-coloured flower and place this in front of or near to your symbol. (There is more on God and Goddess symbolism in Chapter 3, 'Moon Worship?')

✱ Make your own gingerbread men and share them amongst your friends and family. If you are a good cook, or feeling adventurous, you might like to make your own Lammas Loaf, plaited into the shape of a wheatsheaf or in the form of a man.

✱ Make a sacrifice of time and effort for the land around you or the community you live in. As the first Monday in August is a public holiday in the UK, our group will often wait until the weekend after and then go out into the woods nearby and collect litter. We make a family day of this, adults and children working alongside each other and competing to see who can fill the most sacks with rubbish. After we have disposed of this we have a party, or picnic if the weather is good enough, where we share our Lammas Loaf and the youngsters enjoy their gingerbread men.

MADRON

21 SEPTEMBER

Modron, the Autumn Equinox, Harvest Festival

This is the Autumn Equinox, once again a time of balance when day and night are equal. As with the other Equinox and the Solstices, the date of this festival may move slightly from year to year, but many will choose to celebrate it on 21 September. In keeping with the balance of the Equinox, Madron is again the time when we seek balance within ourselves. It is a time for throwing out the old and taking on the new. Although similar in this way to Oestara, the emphasis is slightly different, for Madron is the feast of the Healer, the Bringer of Justice and the Release of Prisoners.

At the Autumn Equinox the crops have been harvested in preparation for the winds and storms of early winter. In earlier times, this was when the people had their first indication of how successful the harvest had been and of how much they would have to live on through the long cold months of winter. In times when battles were generally short and prisoners rarely taken, at Madron prisoners would be released back to their families. This seasonal exchange and return of prisoners makes sense when you remember that only persons of rank or potential exchange value would have been captured. To return them at this time would ensure that they were not extra mouths to feed and would possibly buy the return of your own friends or family before the hard weather set in. Before the advent of our modern roads, travel would have become increasingly difficult after the end of the summer, with rain turning the ground to mud and darker nights cutting short the available travelling hours. In late autumn and winter you might be stranded a long way from the nearest village, or even house, without adequate food or fire for weeks. For the same reasons, at this time of year disputes were less likely to be resolved by combat, bringing a time for the healing of physical wounds and the resolution of arguments.

Today's Witches still mark this Sabbat with the release of 'prisoners', in this case not people held hostage but old regrets and arguments we have held on to over the preceding season. This is a time for forgiveness, of others but primarily of self. Your prisoners are the things that you berate yourself with, such as the mistakes you have made and the things you have said, or not said, which cause you regret and which are holding you back. This does not mean that you simply forget the things you regret, as you may well feel the need to make amends in some way, and this is an important part of the healing process. For example, if you borrowed some money and feel guilty for not having repaid it, even though the person you borrowed it from may not have asked for it back, you will need to repay the money as well as put the guilt aside. In this way Madron becomes a very real occasion of healing, for it is only by putting our mistakes behind us that we can move on with the lessons we have yet to learn.

A MADRON RITUAL

The key themes of Madron are balance – day and night are equal – and it is the feast of justice, of the healer and of the release of prisoners.

A few days before you are to celebrate Madron go out and collect a handful of dead leaves. Take them home and put them somewhere to dry out thoroughly. Give some thought to the 'prisoners', the regrets you wish to release, and for each one, mark a symbol on a dead leaf. As an example, your symbol of the unpaid debt might be a dollar sign. Also consider whether you need to do anything practical, such as paying off that debt, or apologizing for any harsh words you have spoken, in order for your process of healing to begin. Ideally, these practical actions should be performed before you begin your ritual, so that the matter can be completed at the Sabbat, but you may find that some actions cannot be fitted in until after your Madron rites.

When it is time for you to perform your ritual, invite the elements, the Goddess and the God in the usual way.

Now take out your leaves. Look closely at the symbol on each one and as you do so, think about the situation that caused you regret and consider what you have learned from it and how you might avoid a similar situation in the future. Hold the leaf up and ask the Goddess to take this problem from you and to give you strength in the future, then crush the leaf in your hand.

Later you will need to dispose of your leaves. They can be thrown to the winds, placed in a stream, buried in the ground or burned if you have the opportunity, thus casting these problems away from you. If you still have practical actions to perform to put right any problems, you might like to keep back those leaves until the actions are completed. They will act as a physical reminder of the promises you have made.

Having discarded your 'prisoners', you now need to take on some positive thoughts or habits which represent the healing side of this Sabbat. For this you will need a length of white cord. Take your cord and tie one knot in it for each new habit you intend to get into. For example, you might wish to promise yourself that you will pay debts back promptly, that you will try to think before making personal comments or that you will endeavour to think of a positive personal attribute every time you criticize your own appearance. This would be three knots in your cord. You can make yourself as many promises as you wish, but you will find it more effective if you pick three or four main items and focus your intent fully on them, rather than choosing dozens which you can't remember later.

As with all the Sabbats, remember to celebrate the Rite of Wine and Cakes before you close by thanking the elements, the Goddess and the God.

OTHER WAYS OF MARKING MADRON

★ Make a harvest wheel from apples. These days almost all of us can obtain apples at any time of the year, but they used to be a symbol of the harvest and if you cut one open across the core you will also see that they contain a symbol of the Craft in that the seeds describe a five-pointed star.

To make the wheel, take three or four apples and cut them into slices across the core. Make each slice about 4 to 5 millimetres thick. You will need to discard those slices which come from the very ends and those which are too small. Place your slices in a single layer on a cooking rack in a conventional oven on a very low heat until they dry out. Next place them on newspaper in a warm dry place overnight. At this stage you may also need to throw away any slices which have curled too much, although this can sometimes be remedied by placing them under a heavy weight, perhaps a couple of books, for a day or so.

Once your slices are thoroughly dry, arrange them in a circle, so that each slice slightly overlaps the ones before and after. Take time over your arrangement and when it looks pleasing to you, glue the slices into place and leave them to dry.

Once your wheel is completed you can decorate it if you wish, but do try to keep within the theme of harvest. It will need to be hung somewhere which does not get damp as however good your drying process, you do not want it to subsequently start to rot.

☆ Find a symbol of balance. This could be something man-made, such as a Yin–Yang symbol or even a set of scales, the old-fashioned kind with two arms. Alternatively, it could be something from nature such as a stone which is both light and dark in colour or a stick which you suspend from its exact centre. Whatever the item, place it somewhere where you will be easily able to see it. This is a reminder not just of the balance of the Equinox, but also of the balance which we seek in our lives all year around.

☆ Take up a new skill connected with healing. There are many so-called 'alternative' therapies which can be studied and serve as a useful addition to 'conventional' medicine. Aromatherapy, homoeopathy or general herb lore are all good examples. Healing is one of the very basic skills of the Witch, even if you have no intention of practising it on anyone other than yourself. Indeed, you should always ensure you study under a recognized teacher before you try out any 'potions' on anyone, even yourself. However, there are many domestic remedies which are perfectly safe,

such as peppermint tea for a stomach upset or a lavender-soaked cloth for a headache.

THE WHEEL OF THE YEAR AS A WHOLE

The eight Sabbats form the Wheel of the Year, a never-ending cycle of beginnings and endings, each leading one to the other. There is no way to do justice to all of the Sabbats within a single chapter – a book could be written on each one, containing the legends of the Goddess and the God, the traditions and the ways of celebration. One way of celebrating each Sabbat is to spend some time reading up on these legends and traditions, and it is no less valid a way of marking the Wheel of the Year than ritual.

Another way is to make a point of going out into the land and observing the changes of the seasons, perhaps taking an item from the countryside to remind you of each Sabbat, such as an ear of corn for Lammas or a holly leaf for Yule. If you do this, please do so in moderation – it is one thing to bring a token of the festival into your home, it is quite another to strip the land of its resources or to take an endangered wild flower.

Whichever way you choose to celebrate the festivals, it is important to remember to see the cycle as a whole and to look not only at the past, the history and mythology of the festivals, but also to reflect those stories back to your own life. The Craft is a living belief system which you can, and should, use to bring positive change into your own life.

FIVE

BECOMING A WITCH

Thus far I have only talked about Witches in general, but like many other belief systems there are many kinds of Witch. The most commonly mentioned are Gardnerian, Alexandrian, Hereditary, Traditional, Solitary and Hedgewitch. As you will see below, these categories are not necessarily exclusive; one can be Gardnerian Hereditary or Traditional Solitary Hedgewitch, or almost any other combination. There are those who do not fit into any of the above categories and there are those who have taken elements from outside the Craft to enrich their worship and their Magic. The term 'Witch', then, is very hard to pin down, but it tends to be non-Witches who want a 'proper' definition – Witches themselves are usually quite happy to know what they are and define themselves by their actions rather than the impressions of others. Here I have given just an outline of the categories above.

GARDNERIANS

Gerald Gardner is often termed 'the father of modern Witchcraft'. After the repeal of the Witchcraft Act in the 1950s, he was the first author and Witch to write about the Craft and to be relatively open about his involvement in it. Together with Doreen Valiente, he was responsible for some of the major elements of written Witchcraft that we have today.

Gardnerian Witchcraft includes a lot of formalized ritual and quite a lot of working on the astral or psychic plane. Gardnerian Witches follow, quite strictly, the rituals and rites of Gerald's original Coven, and trace their descent, via initiation, from that Coven.

To become a Gardnerian Witch you have to have been initiated by a Gardnerian or by one who is recognized by Gardnerian Witches. You will also need access, whether from memory or through texts, to Gardner's original 'Book of Shadows', some of which can be found in published texts.

ALEXANDRIANS

Alex Sanders came to prominence in the 1960s and 1970s when his flamboyant approach attracted a lot of public and media attention to the Craft, not all of it good! However, Alex's flair and notoriety did mean that the Craft was taking its first steps towards public knowledge and, to some extent, acceptance.

Alexandrian Craft is less formalized than Gardnerian. Its rituals can be adapted to suit people in many circumstances and in this way it is a more open and free-form religion. Access to Alexandrian Craft and ritual can be obtained from the works of Janet and Stewart Farrar, who worked with Alex for a number of years. It is important to remember, however, that not everything has been printed and that not everything that has been printed is 'set in stone'; one of the key tenets of Alexandrian Craft is its adaptability.

Both Gardnerians and Alexandrians practise the three degrees of initiation.

HEREDITARIES

Hereditary Witches, as the name implies, are those whose Craft is passed down through their family. The only way to become a Hereditary is to be born into a 'Witch family', to marry into one or, in rare cases, to be adopted as a Hereditary Witch (the latter does not necessarily mean that the person is also adopted by a couple in the same way as a child is adopted). Most Hereditaries are quite secretive, so that no one outside the family may realize they practise the Craft. Their rituals are closely-guarded family secrets and in some cases bear little resemblance to 'mainstream' or public Witchcraft. In particular their system of initiation may consist of only the one rite, or of a great many, rather than the three degrees of Gardnerian or Alexandrian Craft. There are Hereditary families who pre-date Gardner; indeed, Gardner himself claimed to have been instructed and initiated by a Hereditary Witch.

TRADITIONALS

Another term for Traditional Witch is Instinctual. These Witches are those whose learning and practice cannot be easily traced through either family or Coven practice. There are some who say that there is no such thing as a Traditional Witch; however, there are also those who believe that the Instinctual Witch is in fact one who has been reincarnated with the Craft knowledge from a previous life. Either way, there is no real way to explain how a very few people seem to be born with more Craft learning than they could have acquired through their study in this life.

HEDGEWITCHES

These Witches follow a more nature-based path and their rituals are often less formal than those of the Gardnerians or Alexandrians. Their Magic is often strongly connected with the use of herbs and plants, and frequently takes place in the open or in the kitchen. The tools of the Hedgewitch are more likely to be a good sharp herb knife and a saucepan than an Athame and pentacle. When approached to do some healing, they are as likely to produce a soup or a lotion as they are to light candles and incense.

SOLITARIES

This is the term for those who worship and practise alone, whether through choice or through circumstances. Most of you reading this book may find yourselves in this category. Solitaries may come from, and follow, any of the above paths, or even one of the lesser known ones. A great many Witches start by being Solitary, only joining a Coven when the right one comes along. Indeed, most people who follow the Craft will find themselves working as a Solitary at some time.

COVENS AND HOW THEY WORK

The Coven is the 'family group' of the Witches. It will usually be made up of a number of male and female Witches under the direction of the High Priestess and/or High Priest, although the High Priestess should have precedence.

The Coven will meet at the eight Sabbats and the 12 or 13 Full Moons. Some groups will also meet at the New Moon and this would make 33 meetings a year. Most meetings are conducted in the evening and on the day of the actual event, and although some groups will move their meetings to take place only at weekends, this is quite rare. Members are expected to attend every meeting unless they have a very good reason not to, and they are expected to arrive punctually and be fully prepared.

Outside meetings, members are expected to study their Craft and any specializations within it. They may also be assigned work by their High Priestess. In addition, they will be expected to inform their High Priestess about any Magic they intend to carry out and to keep a record of the results of such working. Many Covens require the keeping of a personal record of rituals and Magic by each member. This is called the Book of Shadows.

As you can see, belonging to a Coven is quite a lot of hard work. For a Coven to operate well, all its members must be committed and self-disciplined. Mind you, this is nothing to the amount of work and dedication that is required of the High Priestess and High Priest. These are the 'parents' in the Coven and it is up to them to provide the training, assistance, care and control that the members need in order to grow within the Craft. It is also their responsibility to ensure that relationships within the group run smoothly and that no one is ever put into the position of doing something they are not comfortable with or sure about.

Nearly all Covens will require potential members to undertake a period of pre-entry training and assessment. This is to partly to ensure that the aspirant is truly making an informed choice of path and partly to try to ensure that they will really fit in. Reputable Covens rarely take entrants under the age of 18 and even then it is likely to be only a matter of months under that age. However, some Covens or High Priestesses will support younger people by advising on reading and activities and answering questions until they are of an age to join.

THE DEGREE SYSTEM OF INITIATION

This varies from one tradition to another and even within traditions. Although three degrees of initiation are usual, there are groups who have more or fewer than this. It used to be the case that the aspirant waited a year and a day without meeting any of the Coven members or attending any of its rituals before taking their first-degree initiation and becoming part of the group. However, many groups now prefer to use an altered form of this. The aspirant joins the Coven as soon as they are deemed potentially compatible, although they are only allowed to attend a limited number of rites and rituals. They then work through a year and a day within the Coven before taking their first degree. This is preferred by many High Priestesses as it is felt this way the newcomers will have a better idea of what they are joining and the group members will have a better ability to assess a candidate's compatibility and sincerity.

On joining the Coven the aspirant is usually required to take a Coven Oath. This is a promise made to the Goddess and the God, and is usually concerned with preserving the secrecy of the Craft and the Coven. The oath-taker is not under any threat from the High Priestess or the High Priest or members of the group, but is required to keep their promise on their own honour. Of course, failure to do so might result in them being asked to leave the group, as they would have broken group trust. The oath of my own Coven reads:

'I, [name], undertake this oath of my own free will, in the presence of the Old Gods and before all here. I will not reveal the secrets of the Craft, nor use the knowledge I gain to impress the foolish, nor to frighten the childish. I will

follow the Old Ways, in humility and obedience, to the best of my ability, and uphold the Craft as best I may. I will not reveal the secrets of the Circle, the nature or detail of its workings, nor the names of its members.'

In traditional groups the aspirant will then be required to wait a year and a day before seeking initiation to the first degree.

The first-degree initiation is simply a statement of beginning and there are many texts of this in published works. Its form will vary considerably from one group to another, especially as there is a current trend towards simplifying some of the older rituals, which have grown unwieldy.

The first-degree Witch will then continue to work and study and in the fullness of time, at least a year and a day later but more normally two years, will take their second degree. This level indicates that they have passed from the stage of simply learning to that of being able to pass on knowledge, but under supervision. The second-degree Witch is in a position to initiate others to the first degree, but only with the consent of the High Priestess, and can run a Coven, again under the supervision of the High Priestess.

Some Witches choose to take a new or Witch name at their second degree; this is the name that they will be known by in the Craft. It is not the same as simply choosing a 'pen name', as many Internet users do, for the Witch name will be one which has special significance for the owner and will encompass skills, talents and abilities which they aspire to. In some Covens the Witch name is chosen by the High Priestess, often in recognition of talents, or future talents, that the Witch may not be aware of.

The third degree recognizes that the Witch is now fully capable and can work without supervision, although it does not mean that they can stop learning. Taking this degree usually means that the Witch now wishes to run their own Coven without the supervision of their original High Priestess, although, generally speaking, assistance and guidance are always there if required.

The period from second to third degree is very variable, being at least a year and a day, but it can be as long as 20 years, especially if the Witch concerned has no desire to take on the running of a group.

Initiation is always passed female to male and male to female, except in very rare circumstances, as this emulates the balance of the male and female in the divine. There is a lot more depth involved in each of the initiations than I have gone into here, but you will learn as you progress through each step. Initiation rituals, whilst published in outline, always contain some elements of mystery – to publish all the information would be to spoil it for the candidates who have not yet taken these steps. Having said that, if you are approaching initiation and have any concerns about the content of the ritual, you should discuss this with your High Priestess, as at no time in the Craft should you ever be expected to do anything which you are not fully prepared for.

Group or Coven working is not always practical or possible, for the following reasons:

★ It can be hard to find a group within reasonable travelling distance, especially as the majority of Covens still do not advertise. Whilst it once used to be quite common for people to stay overnight on the High Priestess's floor, in these days of smaller houses and more extensive work commitments this is not always practical.

★ It can be hard to find a group into which you fit, as it is important in group working that everyone feels comfortable with everyone else and that you can all work as a team. Think of it as choosing the horses to pull a carriage – it's no good having three cart-horses and one thoroughbred!

★ It can be very hard to find the extra time which group working requires, as you need to be able to attend rituals at the times laid down by the High

Priestess. Often it is not the time for the ritual which causes the problem, but fitting in travel time around public transport and family commitments can be difficult.

Solitary working has a number of advantages and some disadvantages:

✴ You do not need to go anywhere to do it. You can work in your bedroom, the garden or even a local park.

✴ You can work whenever the need or mood takes you – you do not need much forward planning, although you do still need to plan your Magic carefully.

✴ Because you are alone, you do not need to wait for others to arrive or to get ready and there is no need to ensure that everyone else is clear about the intent of the ritual. You tend to need fewer tools and less equipment as there is less need for visual keys or links to tune everyone in. If you are feeling unwell you can simply postpone your ritual to another day and no one else will be inconvenienced.

✴ However, you do not have the companionship and support of others who are following the same path and who may experience the same problems and difficulties.

✴ You have no one to share the joy of the Craft and your love of it. Whilst a Coven meeting is not a social activity, there is always time afterwards for celebration and laughter.

These latter two points can often be resolved, at least partly, by membership of a Pagan organization or through networking on the Internet (*see* Chapter 9, 'Getting in Touch').

At this point it seems appropriate that I should give you some idea of my own steps in the Craft. When I was quite young I spent quite a lot of time with an elderly lady who was herself associated with the Craft. She taught me a lot but never called it Witchcraft, she merely encouraged me to see things from other perspectives. This meant that by the time I became interested in the Craft itself, in my teens, I already had quite a good grounding in much of the wisdom and lore.

Unable to find other Witches, I self-dedicated and worked Solitary for many years before taking my initiations in both Gardnerian and Alexandrian Craft. During my years in Coven it became suspected that I might also lay claim to having a Traditional background and evidence for this has come to light on more than one occasion since I became High Priestess of the Hearth of Hecate.

In all I now have nearly 30 years' Craft experience in nearly all of the forms mentioned above and, indeed, have friends in the Craft who come from all paths and parts of the world.

My reason for telling you this is to show that it is not necessarily the simplest path, or even the one first selected, which proves to be our ultimate destination. The Goddess moves us all in her own way.

BECOMING A WITCH

It might seem that becoming a Witch is very complicated, but in essence it is no more complicated than deciding to become, say, a Christian. If you think of the Craft as being in three parts – religion, ritual and Magic – then those can be looked at as three distinct steps. First, if you feel that the tenets and beliefs of the Witch are for you, then you can start being a Witch from that point. The second step is working the Craft. It will take you time to under-stand the various rituals and to formulate your preferred way of performing them, but the guidelines in Chapter 4, 'The Eight Sabbats', and Chapter 7, 'Spellcraft and Herb Lore', will help you there. Magic, the third step, will take longer to understand, and will require a lot of study, effort and practice before you will get it right. The good news is that failed Magic rarely does any harm – it simply doesn't work.

Let us look at that first step in more detail. To recap, the beliefs of the Witch are as follows:

* The divine is both male and female, equally and in balance. There is a Goddess and a God.

* We should respect nature.

* Everyone is entitled to their own informed choice of spiritual path, so long as they harm no one else.

* The Wiccan Rede: 'An' it harm none, do what thou will.'

* The Law of Threefold Return: 'Whatever you do, be it good or ill, will be returned to you threefold.'

* The seasonal cycle is celebrated through the Eight Sabbats and the Wheel of the Year.

* The cycle of the Triple Goddess is shown through the Lunar cycle.

* We have personal responsibility – our thoughts, feelings, words and actions are our own responsibility.

★ We strive for personal development – we should each work towards being the best self that we can.

★ We are each our own Priest or Priestess and need no one else to interpret our Gods or our spirituality for us.

★ We practise divination, finding knowledge by other than our five senses.

★ We practise Magic, making changes by force of will.

★ Life continues after death, with the Summerlands and reincarnation.

If you feel that the above gives a good indication of your spiritual beliefs, then you are already in a position to call yourself Witch if you wish. However, many people feel that simply 'applying the label' is not enough, they want to make some formal declaration. In a Coven this would be their first-degree initiation; for someone working on their own this is called self-initiation or, more correctly, self-dedication.

SELF-DEDICATION

Being a Solitary you do not need to go through the three degrees of initiation; you are, after all, your own teacher and student, and to all intents and purposes your own High Priest or High Priestess (although telling others this speaks largely of ego!) However, you can perform a ritual of self-dedication to mark your choice of path. This can be as simple or as elaborate as you wish. The one below is quite simple, but you can always add to it.

Many individuals choose to take a Witch name at this time. Make your choice carefully – you should be prepared to live with this name for a long time. A Witch name does not have to be the name of a Goddess or God; indeed, to choose the name of a major deity is overly arrogant. Try not to be too obvious. The Craft and Paganism in general are in danger of being overrun by those called Raven, Morrigan, Willow, Morgan and Merlin. You might choose the name of a herb, plant or tree, a country, sea or river, an animal, bird or fish, a mythical place or creature. You can even make your own name from the component parts of others, but watch out for unintentional puns like 'Lunarsea'!

Working on your own you do not need robes, whether plain or elaborate, but many people like to choose an item of clothing or jewellery which they will set aside for their Craft work. This can be a special shirt or dress, a ring or necklace, or anything else which you feel meets your need to mark the change from being your everyday self to being a working Witch. It does not have to be expensive or elaborate – a special pebble picked from the beach and threaded on a cord or a pretty scarf or shawl found in a second-hand shop is as likely to give you the feeling of moving from one mood to another as an expensive new robe or special set of clothes.

At this point you also need to give some thought as to how you actually perceive the divine. Do you wish to call upon the Goddess and the God by name, or as the Lord and Lady? If by name, which names? You can of course refer to them as the Lord and Lady most of the time and only use specific deities and titles when they are appropriate to your rites. But if you are intending to dedicate yourself to a specific deity or deities then you should read up on their stories and be able to imagine them clearly in your mind's eye.

Write your own promise of dedication. There is one included in the following ritual and you are welcome to alter it for your own use, but often it is better if you make up your own words, as a good part of the effectiveness of any ritual comes from the knowledge that your words reflect your intentions precisely.

You will need to set a date for your ritual. Obviously you can choose one of the Sabbats, but you may find that you have to wait a while before your preferred date comes around. Either the Full Moon or New Moon are excellent times for self-dedication. Alternatively you can select a date which has special significance to your chosen deities. There are several excellent books and almanacs which give Goddess and God days, so that you can select a date which is actually one of their festivals. If you do this, you should refer to a Lunar calendar too, as you will still need to ensure that the Moon is either waxing, full or near full, not in a waning or dark position.

THE RITUAL OF SELF-DEDICATION

PREPARATION

As with all rites and rituals, the first thing is preparation. Select your working space with care. It needs to be somewhere where you can rely on being undisturbed. It does not need to be large, but you should have a small work area which can be cleared to serve as your Altar. Ideally this should be in the north of the room. Your room should be clean and tidy. Think of it this way – you are dedicating yourself to the Craft and to the Goddess and the God, and you do not want to invite them to a pigsty, do you?

Gather together everything you will be using in your ritual and make sure that this is also clean. Have your promise of self-dedication written out clearly and to hand. Similarly, any other notes you feel you may need should be clear and to hand in the correct order – you don't want to spend time shuffling through a lot of bits of paper. Ideally, you should commit as much of your ritual to heart as possible, but we all feel nervous and forget our 'lines' from time to time.

Don't forget to prepare yourself. If you can, take a bath and wash your hair. Whilst you bathe, meditate on what you are about to do and also on the Goddess and the God. Once out of the bath, don't go mad with the chemicals and toiletries. Ideally, you want to present yourself in as natural a state as possible and a whole host of ozone-debilitating sprays, lotions and potions will put you at one remove from nature and the world of Witchcraft. If you wish to use a scent, try to make this as natural as possible. Essential oils are great for this, so are herbal infusions (herbs steeped in boiling water, which is then allowed to cool before use).

What You Will Need

(If you cannot use any of the following, have a look at the list of substitutions in Chapter 7, 'Spellcraft and Herb Lore'.)

Altar: If you are working on the floor you might like to use a scarf or silk square to denote your Altar area.

Two candles: One each for the Lord and the Lady. Tea lights are quite good enough. Don't forget the matches.

Incense: A single incense stick is enough. Frankincense, jasmine and sandalwood are all good choices.

Water: In a small bowl or dish.

Salt: A very small amount in a dish or saucer.

Wine: A Chalice or small glass of wine.

Athame or Wand: If you do not yet have one you can use your right index finger.

Your working clothing or jewellery.

Your notes.

THE RITUAL

Having prepared yourself and cleared a small area to work in, check again to ensure you are not likely to be disturbed. Do not yet put on your working clothing or jewellery. Place everything you will need onto your Altar, leaving a working area in the centre.

Stand, kneel or sit in front of your Altar and with your eyes closed, take several deep slow breaths. Take your time, feel yourself relax and when you are ready you can open your eyes.

Now light your incense and, holding your hands one to each side of it, say:

'I call upon the element of Air to watch over me, to guard, guide and protect me during these my rites. Blessed Be.'

Strongly visualize the element – think of cool breezes and strong winds. When you are sure you can see it in your mind's eye you can move on to the next element.

Light one candle and again holding your hands to the sides of it so they will not get burnt, say:

'I call upon the element of Fire to watch over me, to guard, guide and protect me during these my rites. Blessed Be.'

This time you can see the flame of the candle. Visualize fire, flames and a volcano erupting.

Hold your hands over the water and say:

'I call upon the element of Water to watch over me, to guard, guide and protect me during these my rites. Blessed Be.'

Visualize rivers, streams and the oceans.

Hold your hands palms downwards over the salt and say:

'I call upon the element of Earth to watch over me, to guard, guide and protect me during these my rites. Blessed Be.'

While you are doing this, visualize the element of Earth: rocks, stones, soil, etc.

Next, light the second candle from the first and, holding your hands upwards to each side of the Altar, visualize the Goddess and the God. Sometimes it can help to close your eyes to do this. Take your time and when you are happy that you can feel them with you, say:

'I welcome the Lord and Lady [use their names if this is what you have decided to do]. I ask them to be with me, to watch over me and to witness my Rite of Self-Dedication.'

Now you need to read or speak your promise, for example:

'I, [your usual name], call upon the Old Gods and the elements of Earth, Air, Fire and Water to witness that I have, of my own free will, chosen the path of the Witch. I dedicate myself and all my works to the service of the Goddess and the God. I promise that I will not use the Craft, or the knowledge I gain, to impress the foolish or to frighten the childish. I promise to uphold the Craft and the Wiccan Rede to the best of my ability and to keep silent about the secrets I may learn and the knowledge I may gain.'

If you have chosen a new name, now is the time to make that part of your promise:

'In token of my promise I take to myself the name of [Witch name] that I may grow in its likeness. May the Old Ones know me by this name and may I always be faithful to it.'

Whether or not you have chosen a new name, you should now dedicate your special clothing or jewellery:

'I dedicate this [name the item] to my Craft work and to the service of the Old Ones, that it may always remind me of this my sacred promise.'

Take the item and pass it quickly through the incense smoke:

'I dedicate it with Air.'

Pass it very quickly over the flame:

'I dedicate it with Fire.'

Sprinkle it with a little water:

'I dedicate it with Water.'

Sprinkle it with a little salt:

'I dedicate it with Earth.'

Then, holding it up over the Altar:

'And I offer it and my love to the Lord and the Lady. Blessed Be.'

Now you can put the item on.
Next take the Chalice of wine and your Athame. Holding the Chalice in both hands, say:

'This is the Chalice, symbol of the Goddess, the Great Mother who brings love and fruitfulness to us all.'

Place the Chalice back onto your Altar and take your Athame in both hands, point facing upwards:

'This is the Athame, symbol of the Horned God.'

Now transfer the Athame to your right (or strong) hand, holding it point downwards, and take the Chalice in your other hand. Insert the tip of the Athame into the wine and say:

'Joined together they bring forth life eternal.'

Remove the Athame from the Chalice and replace it on the Altar. Place both hands around the Chalice and hold it high over the Altar towards the Goddess and the God. Take a small sip of the wine and say:

'In perfect love and perfect trust. Blessed Be.'

Then replace the Chalice on the Altar.

Dip the forefinger of your right (or strong) hand into the wine, anoint yourself in the centre of your forehead and say:

'With this wine, consecrated by the Goddess and the God, I anoint myself in earnest of the promise I have made this day. May the Old Ones watch over me, guard me, guide me and protect me in my new and chosen path. Blessed Be.'

Now take just a few moments to reflect upon the promise you have made, perhaps having another sip or two of your wine.

When you are ready, you can now clear away. First thank the Goddess and the God. Hold your hands high over the Altar, visualize them and say:

'I, [new Witch name], give thanks to the Lord and Lady for attending and witnessing these rites. Blessed Be.'

Next hold your hands over, or beside, each of the elements in turn, as you did when invoking them, and say:

'I give thanks to thee, O element of Earth [Air, Fire, Water], for attending and witnessing these rites. Blessed Be.'

As you do so, visualize each element departing or fading in your mind.

Once all has been cleared away on the psychic or astral plane, you should clear away on the material plane. Restore your room to its original state – although if it was untidy then you do not need to untidy it again! Put your special item of clothing or jewellery away somewhere safe. Clean all your working tools and restore them to their correct places. Although there is always the (considerable) temptation to have a permanent Altar, this really is not only unnecessary but also a rather tactless way of advertising your beliefs. It should not be possible for anyone other than another Witch to know that you have been practising the Craft.

After your ritual and clearing away it is a good idea to ground yourself. During ritual or working your spiritual self becomes uplifted and it needs to be literally brought down to Earth again. One of the best ways of doing this is to eat and drink something. This is why so many rituals and celebrations end with feasting.

Those of you who have read other texts on the Craft may feel that this is a somewhat shortened form of ritual. However, this form of working is more in line with the old Craft than the modern revival and just because it is not elaborate does not mean it will not be effective.

This, as I have said, is just the first step. Now you have formally declared to your Gods that you have chosen this path, you have to start working at it. No one can be a Witch simply by saying so, you have to grow and learn and practise. Whilst you *are* a Witch, you now have to *be* one. The next steps, those of celebrating the Sabbats and of working your Magic, will require a lot of effort on your part.

SIX

MAGIC

Magic is often defined as 'the ability to make change by force of will'. It is not about blindly following a series of instructions, reciting the 'right' words or having the right ingredients, like baking a cake. It is about harnessing and controlling your own will, or power of mind, to create the change you seek.

It's important to remember that there is a difference between working Magic and performing a ritual. Rituals can be used to celebrate the Sabbats, to honour the Gods, to give thanks for Magic successfully completed and for many other things which are not of themselves Magic. Magic is an act, or acts, which may be contained within ritual, although Magic can also be practised outside ritual. There are some traditions within the Craft which disapprove of working Magic outside formal ritual, but, as almost every Witch knows, there are times when your circumstances will not allow for a great deal of formality.

The first ritual that almost every Witch learns is that of creating the Sacred Space. As I've mentioned earlier, Witches do not usually have temples or even rooms set aside which are the equivalent of their 'church', instead they create their Sacred Space wherever and whenever they need it. The full or formal way of doing this would be to consecrate the elemental symbols on the Altar, invoke the elements, invite the Lord and Lady and cast the Circle. These actions are often jointly referred to as 'casting the Circle'. Once the

Circle is cast, the contents of the ritual will vary, but frequently they will include Drawing Down the Moon, where the High Priest invokes the Goddess into the High Priestess; some form of power raising, maybe dance and chant; the centre, or object, of the ritual, an act of Magic or a rite of passage such as a Handfasting perhaps; the Rite of Wine and Cakes or the Great Rite; a blessing, usually given by the High Priestess.

The Circle is closed by banishing the elements, thanking the Lord and Lady and removing the Circle itself. Feasting may take place either just before or just after the Circle is closed.

As you can see, just casting and later removing the Circle can be quite an involved process and whilst working steadily through all these steps is an excellent way of bringing together a group of people, there are simpler ways of working if you are on your own. There are instructions for two ways of creating the Sacred Space in the next chapter (*see* pages 140 and 142).

But first let us just quickly look at the purpose behind casting a Circle and each of the steps involved in it. The main reasons are to protect those working in it and to provide a way of containing the energies (or power) raised for Magical working until you are ready to release it.

The Altar will have been laid with a cloth of the colour appropriate to the season or purpose of the ritual. On it will be all the items which are to be used within the ritual, including incense to represent Air, a candle to represent Fire, a bowl of water to represent the element of Water, and salt to represent Earth. (On page 133 you will find a list of Magical substitutions so that you can find ways around using anything which may cause a problem with those around you. For example, if someone in the house is asthmatic you can use perfumed flowers or oil instead of incense.) Each of these elemental symbols will have to be consecrated and purified, excepting salt which is deemed to be pure in itself and therefore needs only blessing. There will also be a statue or symbol of the Goddess and the God, and/or a candle or candles dedicated to them. There will be a chalice of wine and a plate of cakes for the

Rite of Wine and Cakes, together with your Athame, unless you wear it at your belt. Unless the Altar cloth has one embroidered on it, there will be an Altar pentagram, symbolizing the combination and balance of the four elements together with the fifth, Spirit, which you yourself bring to the Circle. There may also be an Earth quarter light. Quarter lights are candles, colour linked to the four elements, which are sometimes placed at the four quarters of the Circle (not all on the Altar), and they are most often used when a Coven is working outside. In addition to all of this there will also be the items needed for the working of whatever Magic you intend to do within the ritual, or, in the case of celebrating a Sabbat, symbols of that festival.

The purpose of most of these items is to provide a visual key, so that when everyone in the group sees them they tune in to the same thing. To give you an example of why this should be necessary, suppose I say to a group of four people, 'Visualize a cup,' one may think of their favourite coffee mug, another may think of a golden chalice, the third may think of a tall wine glass and the last may think of their child's yellow plastic animal beaker! However, if I hold my chalice in front of them and say, 'See this cup,' everyone will be thinking of the same thing. Now, if I am working on my own, I do not actually need the cup at all, unless I am planning to put something into it.

The observant amongst you will by now have noticed that most of the items on the Altar and most of the steps in casting a Circle fall into two categories: the elements and the Goddess and the God. These are two of the keys to working Magic, but when working alone we do not need to have visible or physical representations to remind us because they are all around us and they are within us. The Goddess and the God are day and night, light and dark, summer and winter, and can be seen in the cycle of the Moon and the Wheel of the Year. They are also our female and male attributes. The elements, too, relate to things in the world around us and within us, as follows:

Air: spring, morning, the direction of east, the colour yellow, the air we breathe, the winds around us, youth and new beginnings, and our thoughts. One of the reasons why, when calling upon the elements, we start with Air is because thought should always take place before action!

Fire: summer, afternoon, south, red, the Sun that warms and lights us, maturity and our passions or enthusiasms.

Water: autumn, evening, west, blue, the rain, rivers and oceans, middle age, our emotions.

Earth: winter, night, north, green, the rocks, stones and earth we walk upon, old age, wisdom, our physical self and our actions. (North is also considered to be the direction of power for Witches. This is one of the reasons why the Altar is often placed in the north.)

These links are called correspondences and there are many of them. Particular Gods and Goddesses, scents, sounds, other colours, animals, birds, etc., can all be linked to each other. Correspondences are not just attached to the elements – you can find tables of them associated with almost anything. However, whilst it is a good idea to have a look at these if you can, you do not need to commit them to memory or to follow them slavishly. It is far better to start with the basics and then add your own, as your own links or associations will have far more meaning, and hence power, for you.

Understanding the elements, accepting their place within us and in life, and working towards a balance between them is one of the main features in being able to work Magic. This is one of the reasons why some older Covens still put their members through the 'tests of the elements', a series of challenges designed to open an individual's understanding of not only an element, but its place within them. You can set yourself tests of the elements, but if you are working alone it is often more practical, and safer, to use meditation or Pathworking as a way of coming to a greater understanding of them. My own Pathworking tapes were designed with this in mind. The oath taken at first-degree initiation is sometimes referred to as the 'oath of the elements' and I have incorporated something of the spirit of this into the oath made in the Ritual of Self-Dedication (*see* pages 108–116).

Once you have explored the elements and come to understand how they feel to you, then you can begin to summon those forces from within yourself, without the need for a lot of tools or equipment as visual reminders. But before you get to this stage you may need to have some small reminders before you on your Altar, or just around you when you work. In my Solitary days I used to have what I referred to as my 'portable Altar'. In a small silk square I kept a feather, a crystal, a shell and a pebble, and with these I had links to all four elements (the crystal represented Fire because of the way it reflects light). I tied the square up with a red and green cord, plaited from some embroidery threads, to remind me of the Goddess and the God, and the cloth itself became my Altar. Of course I could have used any of a number of other combinations of objects and you can use your imagination to create your own set of links for working Magic.

I mentioned above that the elements, and the Goddess and the God, were two of the keys to working effective Magic. The third is visualization. To visualize is to be able to imagine something and hold that image in your mind's eye as strongly as if it were there in front of you. For some people this comes fairly easily, but most people find that they have to work quite hard and practise regularly to be able to form a picture and hold it in place for any length of time. Again, this is where the use of physical links comes in. If, say, you are working a healing Magic for Ann, then it is a lot easier to visualize Ann getting better if you have a picture of her to work with.

You can also use physical links to practise your visualization. Try spending a few minutes looking at a photograph of a person, place or animal which you know and love, then put the photograph away and visualize the image. You can practise without using a photograph by visualizing people or places with whom you have frequent contact, so that you can repeatedly check what you have 'seen' against the reality. If you do this daily, using different images, you will soon increase your ability to bring to mind things you have seen or people you have met.

The next key to successful Magic is knowledge. Still using the example of healing Ann, it will be easier to work the healing Magic if you understand exactly what is wrong with her and how the physical process of healing might take place. Suppose she has a broken leg, you can visualize the bone knitting together and becoming whole again. If she has an infected finger, you can visualize her white blood cells rushing to the site to remove infection. This is not to say that you cannot simply visualize Ann getting well, but that your Magic will be that much easier to direct if you know exactly where to send it and what it is to do when it gets there. Of course knowledge also means that you need to be precise about what you are working towards.

One of the commonest causes of Magic 'going wrong' is not deciding exactly what it is you are trying to do. One of the sayings in the Craft is 'Be careful what you wish for', as you just might get it! In other words, you might get what you asked for, rather than what you wanted. For example, if you simply work to heal Ann without being specific about what it is you want to heal her from, you might find that her infected finger remains untouched whilst her sadness over the loss of her dog does improve! Or say you want to be noticed by someone who attracts you. Next day you might find your trousers get covered in pink paint. The Gods have a sense of humour too!

Likewise, if you just ask for money you may find that you find a penny on the ground, or that your favourite aunt dies and leaves it to you in her will, or that your car is written off in an accident and whilst you get the insurance money, you still have to buy a new car. It is usually recommended that if you want money it is best to ask for the opportunity to earn it. This is not just a moral issue, there are reasons for it. First, the concept of money is not one which exists in nature, and the Craft is about working with nature and natural forces. Secondly, all Magic involves an exchange of energies – you cannot create something out of nothing – but work for cash is in itself an exchange and therefore a Magic more likely to succeed.

Another reason for Magic not working is a lack of belief on the part of the person working it that the Magic either can or should work. Put more simply, there are some things that we 'just know' cannot be achieved through Magic and there are others which, deep down inside, we believe it is wrong to do. For example, in the first case, very few people are prepared to believe that they can change the wheel on a car by Magic. In the second case, we all know that it would be wrong to kill someone, whether by Magic or any other method. In both these cases the Magic will fail. Of course, if you have enough confidence when working towards the (theoretically) impossible, it is surprising what can happen. While standing at the roadside with your flat tyre, you may find that someone comes along and changes the wheel for you! In this case your Magic has worked, even if it is not in a way which you foresaw.

There is another, very important, reason for Magic not working: some things are just not meant to be. This is often the case with trying to heal those who are terminally ill, as when it is time for a person to move on from this world, nothing can change that. This is something which many people find very hard to accept. However, we have to realize that often the loss of someone we love is something which might be best for them, even though it may pain us a great deal.

In fact working healing of any kind is something which needs a great deal of thought. If you remove someone's pain when they have a broken bone, it may result in them using that part and aggravating the injury. If you work for longer life for someone who is dying, it may result in them lingering in great pain. So you need to consider very carefully what you are going to do and all the possible 'side effects' it may have. One of these which should not be underestimated is that many people will go to a Witch for physical healing and then 'forget' to go to the doctor too! Obviously, the responsible Witch will always ask about, or suggest, conventional medicine as well. Often when working Magic for the seriously ill, the best method is simply to ask the Goddess to care for them and for all those around them. In this way you can leave the decision to the divine, rather than playing Goddess (or God) yourself.

Another really tricky area for Magical intervention is that of relationships, whether your own or someone else's. On a personal front, however much in love you are with someone, would you really be happy if you thought that it was your Magic that attracted them? Well you might at first, but in a few weeks or months you would be wondering if they really liked you or if they were just with you because of a spell you worked. If you find yourself contemplating this sort of Magic, then it is better to consider things like arranging an opportunity to meet or increasing your own self-confidence.

Working Magic for other people's relationships is even more fraught with complications. First, you have to realize that this is an area where you might be interfering with someone's freedom of will. Secondly, you are entering an area where you can never have all the information or enough knowledge. Say someone comes to you asking you to repair their broken marriage. You almost certainly will not know the whole story, as any one individual can only give their perception of the way things are. Quite frankly, even if you can assume that they are trying to be totally honest, they will not know what is, or has been, going on in their partner's life, let alone their mind. There may already be another partner, even a family, in existence, and to work Magic to bring the leaving person back might wreck the lives of other people. Also, you can never be sure of the 'rights and wrongs' of any situation involving two people and their emotions, as it is almost certain that you will only be given one person's point of view. You cannot know just how irritating, or even unreasonable, even your best friend might be to live with! In these cases I usually play safe by arranging for the couple to have an opportunity to communicate with each other. In this way if the relationship is revivable, then they have the chance, and even if it isn't, an opportunity to talk rarely harms.

You may also be approached for a 'love spell'. Most Witches have clients who approach them seeking 'love Magic' and however much you explain that they will feel unhappy knowing that someone only loves them because of a spell, they still refuse to believe it. Again, you also have the problem of interfering with someone's free will, unless both parties have approached you for the same reason. The only way out of this is to state what you are prepared to do, if anything, and flatly refuse to do anything more. The person may be upset with you at the time, but not nearly as upset as they would probably be later.

This brings me to another reason not to work Magic for other people's relationships. Strangely enough, this tends to be the area where, whatever you do, or don't do, it is, sooner or later, wrong. Any number of things can happen. The couple you have brought together get on extremely well, so well in fact that your client tells their partner about the spell and this causes a rift – for which you get the blame. In another scenario, your client gets fed up with their partner for some reason and blames you for getting them involved with the 'wrong' person, despite the fact that they cajoled you into the Magic in the first place. Alternatively, your client's partner gets fed up, in which case of course you're blamed for 'faulty Magic'. As it is in the nature of relationships that some kind of row will eventually happen, it is almost certain that you, and your Magic, will get the blame.

Sometimes the answer to broken relationships can be to ask for emotional healing. Simply asking that someone be given the strength to come to terms with what they have lost and the courage to start afresh is often far more positive than meddling in the affairs of others.

Of course, sooner or later you will almost certainly get the urge to play Cupid. Realistically the only way you are going to get away with this is if neither party ever finds out what you have done. Otherwise, you can't say you weren't warned!

Sooner or later nearly everyone is also tempted to do hexes, curses and revenge spells. I cannot tell you not to do these. Just one thing to bear in mind, though: however just your actions may seem to you, you must be prepared for that negative energy to rebound on you, or someone close to you, three times over. If you are very unlucky, you may find that your 'victim' is also a practitioner of Magic, and possibly a better one than you, and this can start a chain reaction of events which inevitably leads to a number of people being very unhappy indeed.

If you really must get your own back on someone, the best curse of all is simply to ask that they 'get what they truly deserve'. In this way, you can leave it to the Goddess to decide on the rights and wrongs of the situation and what, if any, action needs to be taken. Remember also that working negative Magic is very much against the Wiccan Rede: 'An' it harm none, do what thou will.' Besides, I've always found that annoying and irritating people, if left to their own devices, reap the rewards of their behaviour eventually, and the nastier they are, the more quickly it tends to happen.

One other main category of Magical working is that of protection. These days it seems that an increasing number of people feel under threat or attack. This may be physically, from an angry ex-lover for example, or psychically, either from someone working Magic against them, or from some form of 'entity' they believe to be around. The first thing to mention here is perception. It does not actually matter whether someone is under any kind of threat or attack, if they *believe* they are then that is their perception and the main problem that has to be addressed.

Anyone who feels subject to the threat of physical attack should be encouraged to take practical measures to counter this – improve their security, report it to the police or even move house. But there are Craft measures that can also be taken. Bearing in mind that cursing is not a good option, one of the better measures is to work towards the aggressor moving away, perhaps by doing a spell to get them an irresistible job offer a long way off.

In cases of perceived psychic attack, you need to know that this is in reality very rare. However, it is one of the symptoms of some kinds of mental illness. Obviously you cannot suggest this to your friend or client without the risk of causing huge offence, but do be cautious in your judgement of anyone who comes to you seeking protection from an 'outside force'. Unless you are a psychiatrist you are not qualified to make judgements as to people's mental stability and you want to be very careful not to make any existing condition any worse. There are a number of Craft measures that can be taken against negativity, some of which are included in the next chapter (*see* pages 150–152), however, the simplest is to place a mirror in the window facing outwards to reflect away any negative energies.

By now you may be wondering if I ever recommend working Magic at all? Well, of course I do, it's just that I also recommend thinking about it very carefully and working out in your mind all the possible ramifications that your Magic will have.

I also recommend keeping a record of your Magical, and other, Craft working. If you do this you will be able to see how your Magic works and what the effects are, so that in the future you can refine and improve your technique and ability. Your record is called a Book of Shadows, because what it contains are but the shadows of the real thing. Obviously, if you share your home with others, especially those who are not in tune with the Craft, you will have to be very careful about what you write in this book and how you can keep it away from prying eyes. Regrettably, not everyone respects other people's privacy and if you do not secure your book, you never know which stray visitor or even house-mate will have a look. If you really have serious doubts about being able to keep such a thing safe, then either write it in a code of your own devising or do not keep it at all. Do not be tempted to put it onto the computer hard drive, coded or otherwise, as standards of computer literacy are improving all the time and for some reason people tend to think that computer files are 'fair game', even if they would never dream of reading your diary. In fact a Book of Shadows is a form of diary, for it is the journal of your Magical workings and experience, the place where you record what you did, what happened and how you felt.

If you come to work in a Coven you may find that the keeping of a Book of Shadows is one of the requirements. This is the case in my own group, as I find it an invaluable way of finding out whether my training is up to scratch. Most Coven members find keeping such a record to be a real chore in the first instance, but after a year or so, they come to appreciate the benefits of knowing what worked well and what went less well.

There is a saying, occasionally called the Magician's rules, which really sums up the things you need for successful Magic: 'To know, to will, to dare, to keep silent.'

To know means to work out exactly what you want to do, precisely what change you are seeking to make, and to consider all the possible effects this may have, so that you don't create any unwelcome changes.

To will means that you must apply the whole force of your will, through the balance of the elements and the power of the Goddess and the God. Using the elements means bringing together your thoughts, passions, emotions and physical energy to focus on the problem and its solution, to the exclusion of all other thoughts. Then, using visualization, you direct that force, with all your energy, towards your chosen solution. This is what will make the Magic happen.

To dare means you must actually get on and do it. It's no use just thinking about the changes you want to make unless you are prepared to get on with making them. To dare also means believing that you can work your Magic, as even the slightest doubt in the back of your mind will weaken your will and therefore dilute your Magic.

To keep silent has been mentioned elsewhere, but in a Magical context it is even more important. The first reason is because Magical energy can be diluted by others, especially if they don't fully approve of what you are doing. This is another downside to Coven working. If just one person in the group has doubts about the working taking place, then they can, quite inadvertently, prevent or dilute the energy being directed.

The second reason is because by discussing your Magical working you dilute your own energy. Think about the last time you were really angry or upset and talked about it with a friend. Doing so would have helped to soothe your feelings and calm you down – it diluted the strength of your energy. The same applies with Magic, as you need the whole force of your convictions behind what you are trying to achieve.

There is a third reason to keep silent and that is to protect your own privacy. If you tell just one person that you are a Witch and working Magic, then chances are that word will get out. I once heard it put this way: 'How can you trust your friend to keep a secret, if you can't?'

The exception to keeping silent is when you are working with others, as everyone concerned needs to be working towards the same ends. In a Coven these things are usually discussed before the work begins and anyone who remains unconvinced about the necessity for the working is expected to speak up and possibly even step out of Circle. But you do not always have to meet up to work Magic with others. There is an increasing use of e-mail to inform

other Witches, whether Solitaries or Covens, and to gain their support for joint workings. Generally speaking, the more important the spell, the greater the number of people who will be asked to contribute their energy. This is usually done in one of three ways.

The first is simply to send the energy to the person who is working the spell. This really should be done in a secure Circle as in sending energy, you are directing your unfocused power for someone else to focus and control, and you do not want to leave yourself open to any other drifting energy which may be around. In this case only the person who began the request needs to have investigated the problem and devised the solution. All the other Witches involved, of course, have to have complete confidence in that initiator.

The second method is for everyone to work on their own but towards the same goal. Here everyone will have to have full information and can then make their own decision as to how precisely they want to work. This is probably the best method for Witches who have not met and in particular for Solitaries, as they not only retain control of their energy but also get the chance to practise their technique. Also, if there are any weak links in the chain, someone who perhaps is feeling unwell, then their problem will not affect everyone else's working.

Thirdly, everyone can meet on the astral plane or in an astral temple. This technique is more often used by people who have worked together closely for some time and is often used when one member of a Coven cannot travel physically to be with the others. Astral travel takes a lot of practice and is really best learned from a good teacher or mentor, as there are hazards on other planes of existence which you not only need to be prepared for but also to be psychically guided away from.

In this chapter I have talked about the ways in which Magic works and why it sometimes doesn't. I've spoken about some of the potential consequences and responsibilities, and emphasized the fact that Magic does not need a lot of expensive tools and equipment. However, when starting to work in the Craft, visual keys are very useful. In the next chapter the spells given will centre around such keys, although as you become more experienced you can always choose to work without them.

SEVEN

SPELLCRAFT AND HERB LORE

The dictionary defines a spell as a 'Magic formula'. But, as I have already said, Magic is not simply a matter of following a Magical recipe. In order to make your Magic work you need to be able to direct focused energy at your intended recipient. In the Craft, this energy comes from within you and from outside, from the use of the elements, from the Goddess and the God. So true Spellcraft is not simply a matter of having the right ingredients and following the directions, it is about harnessing and directing the power, or energy, towards your chosen result. In the early days of your workings you may need to have both ingredients and directions, but once you master the Magic you will be able to do away with most of these visual keys and work with the energy in its pure form. Of course, if you are working Magic at the request of someone else, then it is often best to have a visual key, a charm or talisman, to give them, as this provides a tangible reminder of the Magic that is being worked.

In this chapter I am going to give you two ways of creating your Sacred Space, one which uses the tools of the Craft and one which uses none, and is therefore usable anywhere and at anytime. You may want to try both to see which works best for you, or you may prefer to stick with one method until you have mastered it before moving on to the second.

Once we've gone through the creation of your Sacred Space, we'll cover some spells. You will find after you have read, or tried, a few, that there are several themes which start to recur. Once you can see this pattern you will find it easy to devise spells of your own choosing. Here I will give you some visual keys to work with, although as you become more experienced you may find that you do not always need to use them. As I have already mentioned, probably the most important thing about getting your Magic right is to ensure that you fully understand the problem and that you are confident that your solution will not cause any other problems, so don't forget this preparatory ground.

In addition to spells I will also include some herbal work. Herbal work is simply an extension of Spellcraft which uses the natural energies of the plants around us to complement and sustain our Magic. After all, why expend a lot of energy on healing a complaint which can be more simply cured by the use of the right natural remedies?

THE TOOLS OF THE CRAFT
AND SUBSTITUTIONS

The following are tools of the Craft which you will find more often used by a Coven, but alongside each I have included an alternative which is more likely to be used by the Solitary Witch. Of course it is up to you whether you want to spend a lot of money on special equipment, but I can assure you that your Magic will be no less effective if you use a simpler alternative.

Altar: This can be a special table or more simply the surface which you clear for your working equipment.

Altar cloth: This can be as elaborate as you wish or can be a simple cloth. Of course you do not have to have one at all. Alternatively, you can use a cloth as your Altar rather than use a piece of furniture.

Pentacles: Whilst for Witches the pentacle (five-pointed star within a circle) means the balance of the elements of Earth, Air, Fire, Water and Spirit, many people have a very negative image of this symbol. There are two main kinds of pentacle: that which you place on your Altar and that worn as jewellery:

> *Altar pentacle:* This represents both the Craft and the element of Earth. You can have a special one set aside for the Altar, perhaps made of wood or stone. You can create your own by taking a small flat stone and painting the pentacle on one side. This has the advantage that you have created it yourself and it can simply be turned over when it will just seem like an ordinary pebble. You can use a piece of jewellery *(see below)*. You can draw one with salt – although this needs a little practice to get right, it is also 'disposable' and therefore vanishes when you clear away.
>
> The use of an Altar pentacle is twofold: first to represent Earth, in which case you can use some salt or a plain stone, and secondly some Witches use it as a combined centrepiece and/or work area. You do not actually need a pentacle as such to fulfil either of these roles – the element of Earth is a part of you and your working space can be just

that, a space. You certainly shouldn't need an overt centrepiece to remind you that you're working Witchcraft!

The pentacle and other jewellery: Pentacles are worn by some Witches and by some non-Witches as well. You certainly do not have to wear a pentacle to be a Witch; indeed, I had been practising for 20 years before being given my first. If you wish to wear one but do not want to be conspicuous, then look carefully at the various Celtic jewellery designs available on the market. The five-pointed star appears within many as a part of the design. If you wish to wear another symbol of the Craft then there are many to choose from: the crescent Moon, the triple Moon)O(, the hare and the frog, to name but a few. There are also many other items of jewellery which have Craft symbolism but which will draw little or no attention, for example amber, jet or moonstone jewellery all have links with the Goddess.

Symbol of Earth: Although the pentacle represents Earth it is usual to find salt on the Altar as well. However, if you have drawn your pentacle of salt you do not need any more. If you still wish to have a symbol of Earth then a small rock, pebble or crystal is in keeping with the nature of the element and the Craft.

Symbol of Air: In a Coven you will often find loose grain incense, charcoal and a special burner (called a censer or thurible) used to symbolize Air. You can substitute an incense stick, an oil burner (with oil), a flower or even a feather.

Symbol of Fire: The usual symbol is a candle. A tea light or nite-light is a perfectly acceptable and far less expensive form of this. However, you can also use a quartz crystal, which reflects the light of Fire, or a gemstone with a Fire correspondence, such as sunstone or tiger's eye.

Symbol of Water: A bowl of water is the obvious symbol of this element. However, you can use a seashell, with or without water in it.

Symbols of the Goddess and the God: Many Covens will have two Altar candles, one to represent each part of the divine. Some groups will also have a statue or painting of the Goddess and of the God. The alternatives you can use for the Goddess include a stone with a hole in it, a flower or fruit, or your Chalice, and for the God a phallic-shaped stone, a piece of wood (preferably oak or holly), a piece of horn or your Athame.

The Chalice: A Coven, or the High Priestess, will keep a special drinking vessel as the Chalice. This can be ornate or simple. It can be made of stone, wood, metal or glass. For a solitary Witch it is common to use an ordinary drinking glass and if possible to set this aside for ritual use only. I know of one Witch who has been using a plain egg-cup for many years.

One of the best sources of Chalices (and a number of other Craft items) is the charity or second-hand shop, but if you buy a second-hand item, do cleanse it thoroughly before use (*see* page 152 for instructions on cleansing an object).

If you want to ensure that your Chalice will only be used for Craft work, keep it separately from other household china and/or glassware.

Athame or Wand: Many sources state that as a Witch you must have an Athame and that it should be a black-handled knife with a blade nine inches long. This is not so. For a start, many Traditional Witches never take metal into the Circle. Secondly, anything that you cannot accomplish with your finger, you will not be able to achieve with an Athame. Lastly, many places now have understandably strict laws about the carrying of knives.

Many Witches will use a 'knife' made of wood, bone or even stone, sometimes as short as 10 centimetres – these are most commonly found as paper knives.

As an alternative you can use a wand – a piece of straight(ish) wood around about the length of your forearm (from fingertips to elbow), or a little shorter, which you have gathered yourself from fallen wood. Some types of tree are thought to be more Magical than others; oak, ash, rowan, willow, for example. However, all living things are sacred to the Goddess and often you will find that, if you ask the Goddess for guidance when seeking your wand, the wood you gather turns out to have a greater personal significance.

A wand does not have to be decorated in any way, but you can decorate it if you wish. You can purchase fine decorated Wands from shops or by mail order. They may have crystals embedded in them, symbols carved into them and even feathers or bells tied to them, but this will not make them any more effective. It is the wood that you have gathered yourself, together with any work that you have done to it, that will have the most personal power.

OTHER SUBSTITUTIONS IN RITUAL

As this book is written mainly for those who are setting out on the path of the Witch and who may live with others who are not interested or even in favour of the Craft, here are a few suggestions for changes you may need to make so that your ritual does not offend those you live with:

Candles: Burning candles may well cause concern; many people are quite rightly worried about the safety of this practice. You wouldn't be the first person to accidentally set themselves or their room alight – I know, I've done both! Stones are a good substitute. Either you can purchase gemstones of the colour(s) required or you can collect coloured pebbles or plain ones which you colour yourself. Where the ritual calls for you to light a candle, take the gemstone or pebble of the appropriate colour and, holding it up in cupped hands, call upon the Goddess and the God to accept this representation of your intention. For example in the Samhain Ritual: 'I call upon the Lord and Lady to see this stone as the symbol of the old year and ask their blessing upon things past.'

Incense: Using incense can often cause offence – people may be allergic to it, they may not like the smell or the dust, or they may have concerns about the burning of objects in your room. Rather than burning incense you can use an oil burner, or anoint objects with essential or perfumed oils. However, this will still cause a lingering odour, not to mention the fact that essential oils tend to be expensive and perfume oils often have a chemical after-smell. A traditional way around this is to use flowers of the appropriate season. You don't have to spend a lot of money on them, just one or two blooms will be enough. If you can pick them yourself, so much the better, but please choose something cultivated or very prolific – depleting rare wild flowers will not enhance your ritual and may even get you arrested.

Speaking: Whilst in a group environment it is important for you to speak (or chant or sing) clearly and audibly. When alone it is not the volume that you use which is important, it is the intent with which you work your rituals and Magic. The Goddess and the God do not require you to speak aloud – any words can be said in your head.

Wine: Some Witches do not drink alcohol anyway, so you are not alone in seeking a substitute for this. Non-alcoholic wine is an option but far better is fruit juice, preferably something indigenous to your country, so for example apple would be a good choice in Britain.

Cakes: The cakes of 'Wine and Cakes' are in fact a form of biscuit made from three ingredients and cut into the shape of the Crescent Moon. When working on your own it is quite all right to use any kind of commercially available biscuit or even a piece of fruit.

Feasting food: If you are a part of a group then there may be a large celebration at the end of your Sabbat, but I have always felt a bit self-conscious if I have tried to 'feast' on my own. However, a feast is what you make it, so I tend to treat myself to something small which I otherwise probably wouldn't have bought – in my case, frequently chocolate!

Other tools: There are many other things which can be added to the above list, but they are not essential. As mentioned earlier, when working in a group the use of visual keys is useful, but when working on your own you do not necessarily need these things.

As we have already discussed, if you wish you can purchase, or even make, some very splendid tools to aid you in your work, but you do not need to spend a lot of money on tools and equipment to be a Witch. You may recall my 'travelling Altar': a cloth, symbols of the four elements, a symbol of the Goddess and God. This contains what I feel is an adequate Altar, should you feel the need to have anything at all. Whilst it would be nice to also have a Chalice, you can nearly always find a drinking vessel or you can use your cupped hand.

CREATING YOUR SACRED SPACE
WITH TOOLS

To use your tools, you will have to find a time and place when you are certain of being undisturbed. The first step is then to 'centre yourself'. By this I mean to relax your mind to clear it of everyday distractions whilst also focusing it on what you are about to do. Many people find that it is helpful to wash and put on a special item of clothing, then to gather together all the things you are going to need. It can also be useful to do a few breathing exercises; just breathing in and out slowly and rhythmically whilst concentrating only on your breathing can do wonders for your ability to focus.

Lay your tools out upon your cloth. Where you place them is not fixed, although it is usual to place the symbols of the elements around the outside in accordance with their corresponding points of the compass, and it is wise to place any candles, if you are using them, at the back, so you do not have to reach over them. Leave a space in the centre for any special items you need for your actual working.

Having brought symbols of the elements, it is necessary to bless and consecrate them, which is done by either placing your Athame into or onto that item or by holding your hands over each (to the sides if you are using anything hot) and saying, 'I do bless and consecrate this symbol of [Earth, Air, Fire, Water] to make it fit for my rites. Blessed Be.' (If you are using salt to symbolize Earth, remember it does not need to be consecrated, as salt is deemed to be pure already.)

Next you need to summon the elements themselves. In a Coven, this is usually performed by different members of the group in turn moving to and facing each elemental direction and drawing the appropriate invoking pentagram, whilst all perform the necessary visualizations. However, when you are working on your own it is not necessary to perform the 'actions'.

We start with the element of Air, as it represents our thoughts and should therefore come first. Visualize the air itself – clouds racing across the sky, treetops blowing. See it in your mind's eye coming from the east. Remember that Air is our thoughts, it is spring and new beginnings. When you are confident that you have Air with you, say, 'I call upon the element of Air to be with me, to watch over me, to guard, guide and protect me during these my rites. Blessed Be.' At first you may find it helpful to do this with your eyes closed, but later you will find that you can visualize over what you see in the 'real' world. After you have done this for Air, repeat it for Fire (which comes from the south), then Water (from the west) and finally Earth (from the north).

Now you need to invite the presence of the Goddess and the God. Here you visualize the Goddess and the God, in whichever forms appeal to you or are appropriate for your working. I find it helpful to imagine them coming as if from a distance and getting closer. See them as smiling and welcoming. When you are sure that you can see them well, say, 'I call upon the Lord and Lady to watch over me, to guard, guide and protect me during these my rites. Blessed Be.'

The last step in creating your Sacred Space is to cast the Circle. The Circle should encompass the whole of the working space and its boundary should not be crossed during the course of your ritual. This is one of the reasons for careful preparation prior to your ritual. You should not need to leave the Circle to go and fetch anything you have forgotten. If you do have to leave the Circle, you will have to open a doorway in the

Circle, close it behind you and then get whatever you need. On your return you will again have to open a doorway and close it behind you. But to return to casting your Circle, in a Coven this will be done by one member walking the outside boundary of the Circle and, using an Athame, or the Coven sword, drawing a ring of protection whilst visualizing an electric blue light. This ring then 'flows' to become a sphere which encompasses the whole area, not just on the horizontal plane, but also above and below.

When working on your own, you can remain in the centre and visualize drawing the Circle using either your Athame or your finger. Start at the north-east point and draw the Circle in a clockwise direction, visualizing an electric blue light which spreads to form a sphere. As you do so, say, 'I conjure this Circle as a place between the worlds, a time out of time, a place of containment and protection. Blessed Be.' Make sure that the line overlaps at the beginning/end point.

Clockwise is also known as Sunwise, or in the Craft as Deosil, and everything which moves within the Circle should move in this direction. Hence when the elements are called you imagine Air joining you from the east, Fire from the south, and so on.

Now your Sacred Space is complete and this is when you perform whatever working you have created it for, whether Magic or the celebration of a Sabbat. Whilst Magic is something you do not do just for fun and the Sabbats only come round at six-weekly intervals, you will obviously need and want to practise the creation and subsequent removal of the Circle. In order to give meaning to this practice it is useful to have something to do within the Circle. This is an excellent opportunity to meditate on the elements or specific aspects of the Goddess and/or the God. You may have some ongoing cause to which you are personally attracted, such as the preservation of whales or encouraging the spread of the red squirrel, which you would like to work for. Alternatively, you can use it as a time to work healing Magic for the Earth or for your own environment.

Towards the end of your ritual, you may wish to perform the Rite of Wine and Cakes, which is the blessing and consecration of wine and cakes to share the blessing of the Goddess and the God, or the Great Rite, which celebrates the union of the Goddess and the God for the fruitfulness of the land and people. As the two rites are quite similar, although performed for different purposes, here I have combined them, so that in your ritual you can use your intent to direct your rite towards whichever purpose seems more appropriate.

For this you will need a Chalice of wine and an Athame (or the ritual substitutions) and a plate with a cake or biscuit.

Take your Chalice and hold it in both hands in front of you at eye level. Focus on your visualization of the Goddess and say, 'Behold the Chalice, symbol of the Goddess, the Great Mother who brings fruitfulness and knowledge to all.'

Place the Chalice down and take your Athame. Hold this in both hands in front of you, blade pointing upwards, also at eye level, and, focusing on the image of the God, say, 'Behold the Athame, symbol of the God, the All Father who brings energy and strength to all.'

Then change the position of your Athame so that you are holding it blade downwards in your right, or strong, hand. Take the Chalice in the other hand and, lowering the blade into the wine, say, 'Joined in union together, they bring life to all.'

Kiss the handle of your Athame and say, 'Blessed Be,' then put it down.

Take a sip of the wine, reflecting upon the bounty of the Goddess and the strength of the God, and focus this feeling on the purpose that your ritual was conducted for.

Next take the cake (or biscuit) in your left (or weak) hand and take your Athame in your right (or strong) hand. Place the tip of the Athame on to the cake and say, 'With this symbol of the God, I consecrate this symbol of the bounty of the Great Mother. Let their love sustain my spirit as food sustains my body. Blessed Be.'

Replace your Athame on the Altar and take a bite of the cake.

Any remaining wine can be drunk, and cake eaten, as part of your feasting, or if you prefer, you may take it outside later and pour it or put it on the ground as a libation to nature.

Having completed the focus of your ritual and celebrated with the Goddess and the God, all that remains is to tidy away after yourself. This has to be done in two stages, first on the spiritual plane by removing the Sacred Space and then on the physical plane by putting away all your tools and returning the area to its normal purpose and appearance.

The first thing to do is to remove the Circle. Starting again at the north-east point, redraw the same line, but this time visualize the sphere and Circle melting and disappearing. Say, 'I remove this Circle and return this place and this time to their own. Blessed Be.'

Next you thank the Goddess and the God, visualizing them in the same way as before. Say, 'I give thanks to the Lord and Lady for being with me, for guarding, guiding and protecting me, and I bid them Hale and Farewell. Blessed Be.' Now visualize them going away from you, perhaps receding into the distance in the opposite direction to that in which they appeared.

Then it is time to banish the elements. Again starting in the east, visualize Air with all its attributes, say, 'I give thanks to the element of Air for watching over me, guarding, guiding and protecting me. Blessed Be,' and then visualize it fading from view. Repeat this with each of the elements in turn.

Try to make sure that you do this carefully and completely, as you do not want to leave residual elemental influences in your environment. The results are not so much dangerous as inconvenient. I know of people who have failed to banish Water and have had a burst pipe, or who have failed to banish Fire and had electrical equipment fail to work. If you are at any time interrupted in your work, do remember to go back later to banish whatever you summoned earlier, so as to leave the spiritual plane clear for your use in the future.

Lastly, return the physical space to its normal purpose and appearance. Please remember to extinguish any candles or incense extremely carefully and never leave a burning candle unattended, not even for a moment. At this point you should make sure that you eat and drink something in order to fully ground yourself.

CREATING THE SACRED SPACE
ON THE INNER PLANE

Creating your Sacred Space without tools and working purely on the inner plane is something many Witches never really come to terms with. This is partly because it requires a lot more work and, just as often, because those Witches never really have the need to develop this skill. This is a pity, for it enables you to work anywhere and anytime, and, when you are skilled at it, to perform Magic in just a few moments.

To be able to do this successfully you really will need to do some preparatory work in terms of becoming familiar with the elements, their meanings, the way they affect you and the way you personally react to them. You will also need to have knowledge of, and communication with, the Goddess and the God. All these things can be learned with the help of the suggestions in Chapter 6, 'Magic', and through meditation and Pathworking. Remember that you contain all the 'ingredients' of the Circle within yourself: your thoughts are Air, your passions Fire, your emotions are Water, your body is Earth, your spirit is Spirit. If you stand up with your feet apart and your arms outstretched, your body forms the shape of a pentagram. The attributes of the Goddess and the God are your attributes, and the genes for both male and female are within your make-up. It is no use just agreeing with these things; you have to understand them, believe them and incorporate them into your view of yourself. Whilst you are learning to do this, though, you can still practise. For it is the practice of Witchcraft which makes a Witch.

As with all the other rites and rituals in this book, you will need to find a time and a place where you will be undisturbed, not just by people but also by outside distractions. Prepare yourself – if you feel it necessary, bathe, put on your special, or ritual, item of clothing or jewellery. Later you will be able to do without these things, but in the beginning it is helpful to 'set the scene' for yourself. As smell is very evocative you might like to consider keeping a particular scent, whether an oil, perfume or even a soap, for use prior to your work. Settle yourself down in a comfortable position and take a few deep breaths to calm, centre and focus yourself. At first it may help to close your eyes and even to visualize an Altar in front of you.

Now focus on the first element, Air. Think about it and the correspondences that go with it. Think about the winds that blow, soft and gentle, fierce and hard. Remember and feel spring breezes over your skin and through your hair.

Next focus on the element of Fire. Think about a candle, a fire, a volcano. Think of how fire purifies, how it can consume everything in its path. Remember the heat of the summer Sun and feel yourself becoming warmer.

For Water, think about rain, streams and rivers, oceans and storms. Feel the power of water to cleanse, to wash everything away, to make things clean and fresh again. Remember the feeling of autumn rainfall on your skin.

And for Earth, see rocks and stones, hills and mountains and even earthquakes. Feel the power of the earth which endures throughout time. Remember the hardness of the earth in winter and feel the strength and firmness of your own body.

Now seek within yourself for your strength of Spirit. Recall to mind a time when you have stood firm in your beliefs or have stood up for what you know is right and true.

When you first start practising this you will need to build up a picture in your mind, adding pieces almost like completing a jigsaw. After you have practised for a while you will find that you can simply recall the whole picture, with all its strength of feeling and power of thought, almost instantly.

Next think of the Goddess and the God. Here you will need to call upon the mental picture you have already built up through study and meditation. It is often better to build each image in the same way as the elements.

With the Goddess you can start by picturing the Maiden, young, fresh, energetic and enthusiastic, perhaps wearing white or yellow, her hair flowing in the breeze. Then add the image of the Mother, bountiful, generous, dressed in red, holding a basket of the fruits of summer. Now the Crone, an older woman, still beautiful, wise and knowing, wearing purple and shielded against the winter's chill. Let these three images merge if you wish, or retain them as a group. See the Goddess smile in welcome and even hold her hands out to you. Welcome her in turn.

For the God you can see the Hunter, a young man full of vigour and energy, as yet untied by the responsibilities of maturity. Then visualize him as adult, older but still strong, ruler of all he surveys. See the God smile and accept you, and remember to welcome him. Whilst thinking of each of these images, search within yourself and find the parts of you that echo these images, and feel yourself welcome in their company.

Now think of the Circle itself. Instead of stretching out your hand to draw it, try to imagine it starting as a tiny spark within you which grows until it fills your body and then expands to fill an area all around you, becoming a sphere as before. This does not have to be large, but should be big enough for you to comfortably move around in it. Now your Sacred Space is complete.

As before, you then need to perform whatever rites you have built this Circle for. If you wish to incorporate the Rite of Wine and Cakes or the Great Rite towards the end, visualize the God holding the Chalice and speaking the words and the Goddess using the Athame. Allow them to share the wine with each other before they offer it to you.

To remove your Sacred Space you need first to reabsorb the Circle in the opposite way to the way you generated it. Then, recalling the images of the Goddess and the God, give thanks to them and bid them farewell. Banish each of the elements in turn by recalling the feeling of them once they were fully established in your mind and thanking them. Take your time to make sure each has fully departed. Lastly, take a few breaths to restore yourself. If you have done all this fully, you will feel tired, for Magic is hard work, and you will need to eat and drink something to ground yourself.

SPELLCRAFT

Both of the above methods of creating the Sacred Space mention the work itself. This is the Magic or spell you intend to perform. In each of the following spells, I have assumed that you will be working within the Circle, even though in some cases you will need to take something, perhaps an empowered stone or herb preparation, out of it for use.

TO BANISH PERSONAL NEGATIVITY

From time to time we all feel influenced by negative thoughts and feelings. These may be caused by the way we feel about ourselves, the things others have said or an unpleasant experience.

To banish these feelings you will need a small bowl of water and some salt. After you have created your Sacred Space, consecrate the water by dipping your Athame, or finger, into it and saying, 'I bless and consecrate this water to drive out all impurities and make it pure and fit for these my rites. Blessed Be.'

Next, bless the salt, sprinkle some onto your Altar cloth and again using your finger or Athame, say, 'I bless this salt to make it fit for these my rites. Blessed Be.'

Now add a little salt to the water and hold the bowl up towards the Goddess and the God. Visualize them being present and say, 'I ask the Lord and Lady to let this be the receiver of all my negativity, so that I might cleanse myself and become whole once more. Blessed Be.'

Place the bowl down safely, dip the fingers and thumbs of both hands into the water and visualize all negative thoughts and feelings moving through your body, down through your arms and out from your hands into the water. As you do this, be aware of yourself becoming lighter, of losing the weight that has been on your mind.

When you are sure that all is completed, remove your hands, shaking the last drops of water from them into the bowl. Take a moment to centre yourself once more and again holding the bowl up to the Goddess and the God, say, 'I ask the Lord and Lady to take this negativity and through their power and the power of the elements to keep me safe in their hands. Blessed Be.'

This rite is often used in conjunction with others as it enables you to cleanse your mind fully before moving on to other work. If this is the only rite you intend to perform you can now remove your Sacred Space. When all is done pour the 'contaminated' water away onto the earth (not near anything you are trying to grow) or down the drain.

TO BANISH NEGATIVITY FROM A ROOM OR TO CLEANSE AND PROTECT AN AREA

You may sometimes feel that a room or your home has been affected by negative influences. Perhaps you have had someone unpleasant there or there has been an argument. In this case you can use a similar method.

Again in your Circle, consecrate and bless the salt and water as above. Add the salt to the water and, holding it up to the Goddess and the God, say, 'I ask the Lord and Lady to let this water drive out all negative influences. Blessed Be.' Put the bowl safely to one side.

Next take a sprig of rosemary, or a small amount of the dried herb tied in a small cloth, and, holding it up to the Goddess and the God, say, 'I ask the Lord and Lady to empower this herb that it might guard my place from all negative thoughts and persons. Blessed Be.'

Visualize the Goddess and the God directing their energy towards and into the herb, so that it becomes charged with their power. Then hold it between your hands and visualize each of the elements in turn adding their power to it – the earth that it was grown in, the air that stirred its leaves, the Sunlight and the rain which enabled it to grow. When you feel that the herb is empowered, put it to one side.

Now you can remove your Sacred Space. Take your bowl of water and gently sprinkle it around the outside edge of the area you wish to cleanse, moving clockwise or Deosil. You do not need a continuous flow of drops or to soak everything in order to perform this. As you go, visualize the drops joining up to make a barrier which drives negativity out and through which it cannot return.

Finally, take your empowered rosemary and pin it up over the entrance to the area you wish to protect.

TO CREATE A TALISMAN

A talisman is simply a portable object which has been empowered for a purpose. You can easily create a talisman for almost any purpose, say self-confidence, creativity, concentration or protection, using the method below.

First you have to select an appropriate object. It needs to be something which can be easily carried. For this reason a piece of jewellery is often chosen. However, you may not have the money for jewellery, or the inclination to wear it, so you can always select a small stone which can be kept in the pocket or purse. If you purchase something, you will need to prepare the object by cleansing it of all outside influences. You can either place it under running water for five minutes, while visualizing all imperfections being washed away, as already mentioned, or you can place it overnight in the light of the Full Moon, in which case it will be additionally empowered by this process. If you prefer to use something you have found, such as a pebble or even a small piece of wood, it is a good idea to wash it to remove any excess dirt, but you do not need to cleanse it in the same way if you are sure that it has been in the elements and not handled by anyone else.

In your Circle, take your talisman and bless and consecrate it by the same process used for the rosemary in the previous spell, but this time ask the Lord and Lady that it perform whichever function you have chosen. When you are confident that it is ready, either put it to one side if it is for your personal use or, if you have prepared it for someone else, wrap it in a small cloth or paper until you are ready to give it to them. This stops it getting handled before it gets to its new owner.

TO ATTRACT NEW FRIENDS OR A PARTNER

As mentioned earlier it is not a good idea to seek to tie an individual to yourself or to another, however it is perfectly acceptable to ask the Goddess and the God to bring a suitable companion, or companions, your way. In this you are not interfering with the will of others, but are seeking the opportunity to meet those with whom you stand a chance of developing a good relationship.

This is one of those spells where you need to be careful what you ask for. It is no good saying you want someone handsome – they may turn out to be a rat! Try to focus on personality rather than appearance and be very wary of making a 'closed' request. If you find yourself thinking of a particular individual, then please, stop doing the spell. By far the best way to phrase your request is to focus on 'someone I will be happy with and who will be happy with me'.

This spell is one where you need nothing other than your ability to visualize and concentrate. Once you have created your Sacred Space, again visualize the Goddess and the God watching over you. Speak to them in the same way that you would to anyone you greatly respect and love. Ask them, in your heart, for the opportunity to meet and get to know the right person (if seeking a partner) or people (if seeking more friends). Take your time doing this and when you are sure they have heard you, thank them in advance. Remove your Circle as before.

It is customary, when working Magic directly for your own benefit, to also make a 'payment' for this, preferably in advance. So sometime soon after you have worked this Circle, find the time to do something for the Goddess and the God. This can be as simple as planting a herb or flower, or even dedicating a disliked task to them, but do make sure that you really do mean it.

Don't expect your Magic to take instant effect. It is extremely unlikely that the very next person to come along will be brought into your life as a result of your Magic. Think of it this way – it takes time to weave the threads of Fate so that the right person can be brought your way.

This spell is sometimes used by those who are seeking a Coven or a teacher in the Craft.

RECONCILING DIFFERENCES

These can be differences between yourself and another or between two other people. If you decide to work this Magic you have to bear in mind that there is only a limited amount you can do before you step over the line of interfering in other people's lives. But that is not to say that you should do nothing.

Sometimes all that is needed is for both parties to be given the opportunity to speak and to listen with understanding. Obviously, the earlier you can do this in a quarrel, the more likely you are to have positive results.

This is a spell which needs to take place over several days and whilst it is started in the Circle, the subsequent steps do not need to be performed in one.

You will need either a picture of each person (even a very rough sketch that you have drawn yourself will suffice) or an object to represent each and three small pieces of wood (used matches work very well).

In your Circle you need to formally name both pictures or objects. Here I have named the parties Adam and Beryl, but you will give them the names by which they are known to you (which might be a shortened form of their real names or even a nickname).

Take the first picture and, holding it up to the Goddess and the God, say, 'I name this "Adam", by Air and Fire, Water and Earth, and before the Lord and Lady, this is Adam. Blessed Be.' Whilst you say this you will need to visualize each of the elements, the Goddess and the God, as you mention them, so take your time.

Put that picture down, take up the picture of Beryl and repeat the process.

Take the three pieces of wood, hold them up and say, 'These three are the obstacles to Adam and Beryl resolving their differences. As each is removed, so their opportunity to meet, talk and listen in truth, honesty and respect are increased, and if the Lord and Lady will it, so their chances of reconciliation draw closer.'

Place each picture, separated by the three 'obstacles', somewhere where you will be able to leave them undisturbed for three days and nights. This completes the part you will work in the Circle.

On each of the three successive days, at the same time, you will need to remove one of the pieces of wood and draw the two pictures that bit closer, so that when all the 'obstacles' have gone the pictures are touching. As you remove each piece of wood, visualize the two coming closer together. Dispose of the wood by taking it outside and driving it into the ground. Leave the pictures together for a further three nights if you can.

Remember, though, that it may not be intended that these two ever do resume their relationship in the way you hope for. However, you have done your best to ensure that they at least have the chance to communicate and perhaps to be reconciled. Remember not to talk to them, or to anyone else, about this spell, for the reasons set out earlier.

The method of formally naming a picture, or a symbol, can be used for other purposes. Suppose you are trying to find a work opportunity for someone for whom you cannot prepare a talisman for one reason or another – perhaps a third party whose aid has been sought by a friend. You can give an item their identity in order to work this Magic on their behalf. Give another symbolic item, perhaps a coin, the 'identity' of a job offer and bring the two together in the same way.

HEALING

I discussed the pros and cons of healing earlier. To recap briefly, you need to be sure that by performing healing you are not aggravating a problem or prolonging suffering. When you have carefully considered how best a problem may be solved, however, then you are in a position to do something to help it.

The simplest form of request is to ask the Goddess and the God to watch over and help the person (or animal) you are working for. Once again, this, like many of the spells I have given you, leaves the decision-making up to the Goddess and the God, who are, after all, probably best placed to make it.

Take into your Circle with you something which represents the person you are working for. It could be a picture or it could just be something which you feel symbolizes them. Name it in the same way as in the preceding spell and, holding it up to the Goddess and the God, simply ask for healing for them.

If, however, you have a good idea of what is wrong and of the way in which nature would put it right, you can direct your spell in quite a different way. Visualize the person before the Goddess and the God and visualize the natural healing process taking place, driven and enhanced by their power, until you can clearly see the person whole and well again.

I cannot stress enough, though, that anyone who seeks physical healing through the Craft should always seek conventional treatment too. It gives confirmation of diagnosis, and conventional and Craft healing are very compatible.

In cases where the problem is emotional or spiritual, perhaps when a person is overcome with grief, then the healing process you are visualizing relates to the process of coming to terms with their loss and achieving personal balance.

EARTH OR NATURE HEALING

Almost every Witch has a pet cause or environmental problem they feel particularly concerned about. This could be cruelty to animals, the plight of the dolphin or an endangered species or simply the overall damage to our planet. Whilst it is not really within the power of any one Witch to cure such global problems, the work that each of us performs does make a difference. Our Magical work contributes towards reversing the trends and bringing back nature's balance. Where we direct our energy towards assisting an organization already committed to solving the problem, perhaps by working towards making their views heard, we can often find that a little Magic goes a long way.

One of the most potent ways of providing Magical assistance is often called 'Raising the Dragon'. In your Circle, visualize a great dragon curled up inside the planet. Take your time envisaging its appearance and, if you can, colour it in sympathy with your chosen cause.

Call to it with your heart and mind and empower it with your energy, wake it and when you feel that you have its attention, tell it of the problem and of the results you would like to see. Tell it also that you are asking it to contribute its own energies and that once it has worked its own Magic that it may return, with your thanks, to its home.

Then, with all your strength, get it to rise out of its lair and flying clockwise, or Deosil, to go to the problem. Once you have released the dragon, watch it with your mind's eye and you will see it fly around the globe three times. Once it begins its descent to the land you may release the image, as your part is done.

Remember to be careful what you wish for and choose a specific problem – do not simply work for 'the good of the planet'. After all, one way of healing Mother Earth might be to remove all the people!

Do not perform this ritual more than once a month, as it can, and should, require a lot of personal energy and to do it too often will almost certainly result in you becoming drained.

There are many books of spells available and some are filled with detailed lists of what you will need to make your Magic work. However, the Magic comes from within you, from your knowledge of the elements, the Goddess and the God. It works through your ability to concentrate and focus, and to visualize. These are the techniques you need to practise. The other things which will enhance your Magic are the use of the appropriate times of the Moon and, particularly when working for yourself, the use of herbs and other plants.

HERBAL WORK

The use of herbs and plants is an integral part of the Craft and is a practice which goes back many centuries. Whilst it would take a lifetime to learn all the healing and Magical properties of plants, it is a good idea for any aspiring Witch to make a start with some of the more common ones which can often be found in the store cupboard or garden, or in many off-the-shelf products. Here I have included just a few of the more easily available useful plants and herbs and some of their properties – a sort of 'beginner's guide' if you will. Careful use of these, whether on their own or in combination with each other, will enable you to create some of the more commonly needed remedies.

Each of the remedies in this section will work through the power of the plants themselves. However, if you Magically empower them in your Circle you will greatly increase their effectiveness.

There are many ways of obtaining your herbs. You can grow your own and if you do this you can be certain of the purity of your ingredients, they won't have been handled by anyone else, and you can empower them your-self, even as they grow. You can purchase a good number of herbs fresh or dried in the supermarket or other high street stores. Some herbs are available as teas, or even tea bags, which is useful where they need to be consumed or if you are making a thin concoction such as a hair rinse. Do not consume any herb which does not come in a form designed for such use, i.e. a tea or food product, unless you are very knowledgeable about all its effects.

These days we can also purchase essential oils which contain the concentrated essence of a plant or flower and which can be added to commercially available lotions, creams, etc., to provide us with a simpler way of producing the results which took our ancestors a lot of time and effort. Good-quality essential oils are initially expensive, although as you only need one or two drops to achieve your intent, they will last a long time if carefully stored in a cool dark place. They will also allow you to avoid spending large amounts of time distilling fresh or dried herbs into a base which can be used. The two main oils which it is certainly worth investing in are lavender and tea tree.

Herbal work is like all other forms of complementary medicine in that it really should be used in addition to conventional medicine, not as a replacement. Also, please remember that this book, like many others, does not make you a qualified herbalist. When you are trying remedies, follow the directions and always start with very dilute forms, as even the safest herbs may bring about an allergic reaction. And never experiment on someone else – you don't know what they may react badly to.

LAVENDER

Lavender cools, soothes and heals. As an oil it can be gently massaged into the temples to reduce stress or to relieve a headache. The plant, flowers and finely cut stems can be made into a lavender bag which can be placed under the pillow to aid rest and sleep. Such a sachet can be suspended, out of reach, over the cot of a small child to encourage a restful night for both parent(s) and child. Either the oil or the flowers can be added to a bath to aid all kinds of healing as well as relax both the mind and body. The scent of lavender reduces fear, anxiety, negativity, mood swings, nerves, worry and much more. A brew made from the herb and allowed to cool will improve the condition of both the skin and hair, relieve insect stings and reduce bruising and swelling. You can see why this is one of the best all-round herbs to use. If you can, grow your own lavender in your home or garden.

TEA TREE

This is the antiseptic essential oil. It can be purchased neat and is found in many manufactured products. Tea tree is used to combat infection, whether bacterial or fungal, and can be of great help with infections such as acne, athlete's foot and thrush, or simply to cleanse a wound to help prevent infection. Like almost every essential oil it really must be used in dilution, either in a base oil or by adding a couple of drops to some warm water.

ROSEMARY

This enlivens and can be used to aid concentration. In ancient Greece students used to wear wreaths of rosemary around their heads when taking examinations, although you may prefer to carry a more discreet sprig or pin one to your clothing. A tea made from rosemary and allowed to cool makes an excellent hair rinse, which can help to clear oily hair or dandruff and will enliven the colour of dark hair. When a couple of drops of rosemary oil are added to a bath, together with rose and rosewood oils, this is a great restorative, and excellent for 'the morning after the night before'. Adding fresh rosemary to your bath is thought to promote youthfulness. Small sprigs of rosemary can be hung in the house to help protect those within against negative influences and conflict. Rosemary on your Altar will help to keep you focused and keep away unwanted influences.

CHAMOMILE

Use the cooled tea as a hair rinse for fair hair. Drunk as a tea, it helps calm the nerves and is an excellent aid to digestion. Cooled weak chamomile tea is often given to infants to aid sleep, reduce wind and even to reduce tantrums. This is one of a number of herbs which can be used as a steam bath for the face and will help alleviate greasy skin and acne. Simply place the herb in very hot water, place a towel over your head and the bowl and steam for five or so minutes. The oil or crushed flowers can be worn to reduce impulsiveness and stress-related anger. Chamomile is a great purifier and can be burned to break bad habits and even to drive away the negative thoughts of others.

PEPPERMINT

Available in tea bags, this is excellent for any digestive problems, including sickness, wind and diarrhoea, and can be given safely (if weak and cool enough) to almost everyone. A stronger tea makes an excellent foot bath, relieving hot and tired feet as well as making them smell good! Peppermint is an aid to concentration and study, and if you carry some of the fresh leaves, you can always pinch one and smell it to give your mind a boost. Use it in this way or rub the leaves on the insides of your wrists just before working ritual or Magic and it will increase your energies.

PARSLEY

Taken as a tea, parsley is a diuretic and anti-spasmodic, and as such can be very helpful if taken for a few days prior to the onset of menstruation. Eaten fresh and raw, the leaves are the best breath freshener available, removing even the smell of garlic or raw onion! For a purifying bath, perhaps before a major ritual, put a few leaves of parsley in the bath. If you have to use the dried herb, put it in a tea strainer and run the hot water through it, otherwise you'll end up with lots of bits to wipe out of the bath!

ONION

Onions reduce fever, infection, swelling and are a traditional remedy for sore throats. I think one of the nicest ways of using them is to make a French onion soup, and if you add a little garlic and parsley to this you have a recipe which can be very effective in reducing the symptoms of a cold or 'flu. The cut edges of onion can be rubbed against a bruise or scratch to remove infection and promote healing, however don't rub it into any significant cut as it will sting. It is thought that placing an onion under your pillow will aid prophetic dreams. Place onion halves or quarters around the house to reduce negativity and quarrels.

GARLIC

A lot of people shy away from eating garlic as they feel it will make their breath and even their skin smell. It can do, but there are ways to reduce this. First, always cut or slice the garlic with a sharp knife, do not crush it. Secondly, eat it regularly, as your body will actually build up a tolerance, and lastly, chew raw parsley after your meal. Garlic cleanses the blood and is very helpful in the treatment of any kind of infection. A paste of garlic rubbed into the affected part of the body will draw swelling and pain, although it will smell very strongly. Garlic is used Magically to protect and to repel all kinds of negativity, including, in fiction, vampires and demons!

THYME

Made into a tea, thyme helps digestion and can ease wind. It can also be drunk last thing at night as it is a mild sedative which relaxes the body whilst

uplifting the mind. It is both antiseptic and disinfectant and can be used to bathe all kinds of wounds. Used as a facial steam bath, it helps clear coughs, colds and chestiness. The fresh herb can be worn to increase psychic powers, to promote courage and give energy. It is also supposed to make the wearer more attractive.

SAGE

Made into a tea, sage is a good all-round tonic and also a remedy for cold, fevers and general aches and pains. The cold tea can be used as a gargle or mouthwash and will relieve a sore throat. Sage was believed to strengthen memory and increase wisdom. As it is a very pleasant herb it can be added to a variety of foods in either the fresh or dried form. As a facial steam bath it will help reduce the symptoms of sinusitis and a head cold. It is also considered to stimulate the metabolism and thereby increase energy, as well as aid in weight loss. Place sage leaves under your pillow to make your dreams come true.

DANDELION

In the garden dandelion is a weed, but in the Witch's kitchen it has many uses. Young leaves can be added to the salad, made into a tea or even cooked in the same way as spinach. Dandelion is an excellent diuretic and an aid to digestion. It is full of vitamins and minerals and will act as a general 'pick me up' if taken daily for a week or so. The roots can be used as a coffee substitute and are said to increase psychic ability. A lot of folklore surrounds the dandelion, including the children's game of telling the time from the seed heads – the number of times you have to blow to remove all the seeds will give you the hour. But you can also use the seed head to send a message to a loved one.

Focus on the person and on what you wish to say, then blow the message to them as you blow the seeds off the head.

EMPOWERING HERBS

You need to empower the herb prior to doing anything else with it as in most cases, a tea or infusion is at its most effective immediately it has been prepared.

If you have not grown the plant yourself, then if you have time, place it in the light of the Full Moon for one night to enhance its energies. I usually find it easiest to put the amount I intend to use in a clear glass and place that on the inside of my window (not the outside as it may fall off). If you have grown the plant yourself outdoors then you do not need to do this as unless there has been no Full Moon since it was planted, it will not have been handled or processed since its last exposure.

Create your Sacred Space in the usual way, with the glass of herb on your Altar, together with a small piece of cloth large enough to contain the herb and a piece of thread.

Once the Circle is cast, hold the glass and herb up to the Goddess and the God. State your intention, whether Magical or to enhance the natural properties that you have chosen the herb for, and ask the Lord and Lady to enhance the herb through their power, and through the powers of Earth, Air, Fire and Water.

Once you are certain that this has happened, place the herb onto the cloth and tie it into a small bundle ready to be used later. If you are

doing more than one, remember to label your bundles or identify which is which in some other manner.

Clear away your Sacred Space in the usual way and then your herb is ready for use.

It is best to use your empowered herbs as soon as you can, as fresh herbs start to lose their potency very quickly and even dried herbs will deteriorate quite rapidly. The only exception to this is a plant's essential oil, if kept in its own glass bottle and in a cool dark place.

This is just a sample of the plants you can use and just some of their uses. Exploring the world of herbs and plants can be very exciting and is certainly rewarding. There are many excellent books and guides which will help you to pursue your herbal work, just a couple of which you will find mentioned in the list of recommended reading.

EIGHT

OUT OF THE BROOM CLOSET

No matter how careful or cautious you are, sooner or later you will want to tell at least some of your near and dear about your interest in the Craft. Alternatively, you may find that the option of being more open may be thrust upon you by circumstances beyond your control. This point, often jokingly called 'coming out of the broom closet' can be a fairly traumatic time for everyone concerned. Now as a Witch you have decided to try to do no harm, and certainly not to anyone you care for, so it is best to consider what may happen and how best to deal with it before the event.

The most common ways to be discovered as a Witch are leaving evidence of your workings where others can find it, finding the person you told 'in confidence' assumes that someone else knows and lets something slip, your bookshelf becomes so obviously 'Witchy' that anyone would notice, you feel morally obliged to come to the defence of the Craft because of an outside event or outside publicity, or an intuitive family member or friend asks the question, even with no evidence, and you give the game away.

First, I would remind you that if you do not want it to be known that you are practising the Craft, then the solution is very much in your hands. Do not tell anyone, anyone at all, anything about your beliefs or your practices. For once you have told one person, the secret is out of your control. Be tidy with your tools, equipment, books, notes, etc., and always clear away after yourself, immediately, after every working. Never work anywhere other than inside your head if there is the slightest possibility that you may be noticed. This means you will have to be very self-disciplined indeed, for watching everything you say and do, all the time, is something few people can really keep up.

Secondly, I would remind you that, as Witches, we do not thrust our beliefs into other people's lives, however much, or especially, if we care for them. So whilst it is one thing to want to share your new-found beliefs and to be honest with those you love, you have also to bear in mind that they may not want to know, whether consciously or subconsciously. For this reason I tend to favour the approach of preparing for the potential questions which lead you to think someone has an interest in what you are doing whilst not actually ever opening the subject yourself. This sounds like being deliberately deceptive, but is the only way I know of which allows people to turn a blind eye if they wish to, whilst preparing to be honest if questioned.

One of the key things that you can do in preparation is to start by living your life according to the principles and beliefs of the Witch. You may be seen to be following the Wiccan Rede (i.e., trying to harm no one) and to care for the people around you or your planet and community. You may appear less judgmental about others and less inclined to talk the rights and wrongs of their actions. In this way you are showing by your actions that following the Craft is not a negative thing. This may all sound a bit 'goody two shoes', but there is nothing so good as showing by example.

When someone makes a comment or asks a question, you will have to use your judgement as to whether they are serious or not. If you feel that they are not serious, perhaps making light of your interesting books or other objects, then you can simply respond with a humorous comment. For example, if they say, 'It's all very witchy in here, isn't it?', you can always answer by saying, 'Yes, looks good, doesn't it?' and leave it at that. There is no need to see a potential confrontation in every passing comment.

However, if you feel that the question has more behind it or the person pursues the subject, I have included an open letter *(see below)* which you may feel you wish to give to someone whose interest seems to have depth. Please be aware that simply handing over the letter in response to the first question or comment is probably not your best move. To start with, it implies that you are either not able or, worse, not willing to answer questions yourself. It also implies that you are avoiding the discussion. The key things in holding such a discussion are:

✯ Do not lose your temper, whatever the provocation.

- ✩ Do not drag in outside issues or allow others to introduce them – if you failed to do the washing up last week, it has little or no relevance to your choice of spirituality.

- ✩ Do listen to another's point of view and answer their points to the best of your ability.

- ✩ If you don't know the answer, say so. It is better to seem to be ignorant than to be discovered making things up.

Remember, these people care for you, so treat them and their views with the respect you would like to be shown to you and your views. If they insist on bringing in 'outside experts', such as books or even a minister, ask whether you might also be allowed to introduce another point of view and suggest that they read some of the books or visit some of the websites which support the Craft. Do not, however tempting, run down another's spiritual beliefs, rather maintain that there is plenty of room for many different belief systems, of which the Craft is just one. As an aside, if you find yourself approaching this kind of discussion with anyone who does not have a good reason to be concerned about you, then politely but firmly change the subject.

A SAMPLE LETTER TO HELP YOU EXPLAIN YOUR CHOSEN PATH

You can use this letter just as it stands if you wish, but I think that you will find it much better to put it into your own words. The first reason for this is that you will be giving it to someone who is probably familiar with your way of expressing yourself and they will know immediately that you are using someone else's words, which is neither polite nor the point. This is supposed to be *your* letter, expressing your views. The second reason is that you may find yourself having to discuss parts of the letter and it will be far easier for you to do this if you have actually given some thought to what you are trying to say, as well as how you are saying it. If you tailor the letter to the person you are writing to, you have a far better chance of them reading it fully and understanding exactly what you are trying to say. You may find that re-reading Chapter 2, 'Witchcraft in Reality', will help you here.

Try not to draft your version of the letter when you are tired, angry, upset or ill and especially not if you are under the influence of anything which may cloud your thoughts and judgement – this could be anything from alcohol to cough medicine, from antihistamines to exhaustion.

Don't forget to use your Craft in preparation for the writing and delivery of the letter. Use the Pathworking technique to ask the Goddess and the God whether this is the right time to do this, whether your wording is likely to be understood, what the potential outcome of someone reading this is likely to be, what questions the recipient is likely to have and any other questions you feel that the Old Ones can help you with.

Whilst you are writing, try to keep a picture of the person you are writing to in your mind. Make this an image of them receiving it in a positive frame of mind.

When you have written your letter, sleep on it. I mean this literally – put it under your pillow and ask the Goddess to guide you. In the morning, read it again and you may well find that her guidance allows you to reword things in a better way.

Dear [Name]

I hope you don't mind that I have decided to write this to you, rather than trying to explain myself face to face. It's just that I find it easier to express myself in writing, so that I can think through what I am talking about. Of course I am happy to talk about this with you, once you have read this letter, but I would like to explain myself carefully in the first instance.

As you may be aware, I have been doing a lot of thinking about God and religion lately. It seems to me that there are many religions in the world, with different Gods, some even with Goddesses, and they all have many things in common. Mainly they promote positive social and moral attitudes which enable us to get along with each other in a better way, such as being kind to one another, caring for those who are less able, respecting one another. It seems to me that there is no reason why these differing beliefs should not be able to be practised alongside each other, if everyone is prepared to be tolerant. In fact a great many wars and other troubles could have been avoided in the past if religious tolerance were more common. I have looked at some of these belief systems and have given it a great deal of thought, and now I feel that I have found a spiritual path which answers my needs, although I accept that it might not be the choice of everyone.

One of my reasons for writing rather than talking about this is because I would like to explain why I find my choice of path right for me. It encompasses many beliefs and I would like to briefly tell you about them:

I believe that everyone is entitled to make their own informed choice of spiritual path, so long as it does no harm to anyone else.

I believe that the divine is both male and female equally and in balance, and that I can find a similar balance within myself. I also believe that I can relate directly with the divine as I see it and do not need others to intercede on my behalf.

I believe that we should respect nature and not take more than we need from our world.

I believe that I am responsible for my own development, that I should work to become the best person I am capable of being.

I believe that I am responsible for my own thoughts, feelings and actions, that I can blame no one else for them. I do not believe that I can blame any outside force for anything wrong I might do.

I believe that I am capable of making positive change in my life and in the world around me.

I believe that, whatever I do, I should always try not to harm anyone else, although I should also strive to be true to myself.

The name of my chosen path is Wicca, which has also been called Witchcraft, and please, before you react with surprise or even horror, can I ask you to read on a bit further. Wicca is one of the older nature religions which were practised around the world before the coming of other, more patriarchal religions. Unfortunately it has been given a very bad name both during the times when it was being superseded and more recently by the media, who have sought to sensationalize it. I realize that you may have a number of concerns about my choice of path and I would like to try to reassure you about some of the more common, but inaccurate, stereotypes.

Contrary to popular belief, Wicca has nothing to do with Devil worship or Satanism. I do not believe that there is a 'negative God' whose purpose is to balance out the 'good God', but rather that I am responsible for anything I may do, or say, and that it is up to me to try to put right anything I may do wrong. I am not saying that I do not need the help of the divine to assist me, but that the responsibility is mine.

Neither is Wicca about the use of drugs, nudity or casual sex. To use drugs would not allow me to develop myself to the best of my ability and my belief that I should harm no one includes harm to myself. The union of man and woman is considered to be a sacred part of a

loving relationship and not something to be undertaken lightly. One of the key points of this faith is that no one should be asked or encouraged to do anything which they feel uncomfortable with and I hope that you will feel enough trust in me to believe that I will use my personal judgement in these areas, just as I will in the non-spiritual side of my life.

This is not just a passing phase, nor something I am doing to shock you, but is a real choice I would like to explore. You may feel that this is something out of the ordinary, but Wicca is in fact one of the faster-growing religions in the world today and there are many others who feel as I do. If you would like I can put you in touch with some recognised organizations, both Wiccan and independent, who will explain further, and who have much expertise in answering the concerned questions of friends and family.

I would also like to emphasize that I am not doing this because I have been coerced or 'brainwashed' by anyone else. No one has forced me to explore this path, nor am I obeying someone else's instructions. In keeping with the principle of freedom of spiritual choice, I really have thought about this for myself.

Also, I really have not done this to upset or worry you, as I know that you care for me, as I do for you. I am hoping that you are still reading this and that even if you do not agree with my choice of path, you are prepared to give me the opportunity to try to answer your questions and concerns. I cannot claim to have all the answers, but hope that, if you are still worried, you will give me the chance to set your fears at rest.

With my love
[Your name]

Before you hand this letter over, make sure that you really want to take this step at this time. You may feel that you have no choice, but quite often we can find ourselves committing to an action which, with hindsight, would have been better put off. This letter is very much a 'one-way street' – once you have delivered it, it will be almost impossible to recall.

If you are certain that you want to proceed, then make sure that you choose a good time to hand the letter over, not when the recipient has a dozen other things on their mind or is suffering some other stress. In these circumstances, you are unlikely to receive a positive hearing. And please do check that you are doing it for the right reasons, not because they have upset you or because you have jumped to a conclusion about their interest in the Craft. Please resist the temptation to watch them or stand over them while they read your letter. You gave yourself time to write and phrase your thoughts, give them time to read and phrase their response. If you do not, you will probably end up with their first, and unconsidered, thoughts!

Do not, however, simply vanish. Try to make yourself available to discuss the issues if the other person wants to. Be aware that their initial reaction may not be exactly what you had hoped for. You may only be able to convince them of your sincerity by showing commitment, patience and tolerance over a period of time.

If the person you have sent or given this to decides to take you up on the offer to put them in touch with outside organizations then I would suggest that you give them the details of The Pagan Federation and the organization Inform, a totally independent body whose details are at the end of Chapter 9, 'Getting in Touch'. If they are prepared to read further, then why not let them read this book?

NINE

GETTING IN TOUCH

Whilst working as a Solitary Witch has a number of advantages, most people, sooner or later, want to meet other Witches. There was a time when the only way to do this was to track down and then join a Coven. This was difficult, as most Covens were quite secretive, as many still are. These days there are, however, other options. You can meet other Witches at fairly open Pagan events all around the world or you can contact Witches and Covens through the Internet. There are advantages and disadvantages to all three ways of making contact, and a few risks, too, but let's look at them one by one.

JOINING A COVEN

It used to be very difficult to find a Coven, as Witches were understandably cautious about letting themselves to be known. It is still not easy, but there are organizations which can help.

The Pagan Federation (PF) provides a way of meeting Pagans of all paths. Some Covens advertise in *Pagan Dawn*, the magazine of the PF, or in the regional newsletters which are available to members. The PF, although started in Britain, has branches and contacts world-wide.

In the UK, there is an organization called the Children of Artemis which helps seekers find reputable Wiccan Covens. Similarly, in the States, The Witches' Voice tries to assist genuine seekers (*see also* the addresses at the end of this chapter).

Hardly any reputable Covens will accept members under the age of 18, although some are prepared to correspond with and support those who are a little younger. If you are under 18, and certainly under 16, and you are offered membership and/or initiation into a Coven, you need to ask a lot of questions. I would advise talking to at least one other member of that group of your own age to find out exactly what they do and don't do. See how the person or people running the Coven feel about the prospect of discussing this with your parents – if they are unhappy about the idea, then they probably have something to hide. Remember, no true Witch will ever make you do anything you are uncomfortable with. I am not saying that everyone who accepts under 18s is necessarily practising a deception, but that the ethos of not encouraging the young is very strong in the true Craft. Just be aware that there are a few highly unpleasant people out there who masquerade as Witches and use the Craft for their own ends. These are not people you want to get involved with.

Another thing to watch out for is people who charge a lot of money for Coven membership or for training. Whilst it is reasonable to expect to contribute to the expenses of the group – wine, candles, incense, tea, coffee, etc. – it should not be overly expensive. In my own group it worked out at just under £2 per meeting in 1999 and that covered Sabbats, Esbats (Full Moons) and New Moons.

ATTENDING PAGAN AND CRAFT EVENTS

You can find out details of Pagan events from the Pagan/New Age press (I will not list such magazines here as they change with astonishing regularity), the Internet and from those New Age stores which have a notice-board of listings. You will need to be patient and persevere in your search, as events are difficult and expensive to organize and so do not happen all that often. If you search carefully, you will usually find a notice of one such event within travelling distance per year. (Most Pagan events are open to people under the age of 18, although some may ask for proof of parental approval before they allow you to purchase a ticket.)

The content of such events, often called conferences, will vary from event to event, so don't be afraid to ask for an outline of the programme before you commit your cash or yourself to a lot of travel. Generally, you can expect to find some talks or lectures, some music and some stalls selling things of interest to the Pagan community.

Most Pagan events will have a Craft presence, if only because around half of all Pagans today are Witches. However, this presence may not be obvious, or advertise itself, so you may well need to make some enquiries. This is the hard part; we all feel a bit conspicuous asking a total stranger if they can point out a Witch who might be prepared to have a quick word, especially when we may have to ask the question of a number of individuals before finding a contact. You also need to be prepared to encounter a certain amount of suspicion here, as Witches on the whole have concerns about journalists and may be as uncertain of you as you are of them. Be prepared to be asked to leave your contact details, rather than being given the details of someone you may get in touch with. This is one of the ways in which

Witches protect themselves from the attention of those they would rather not discuss the Craft with.

Also, please try to be considerate when you do ask your questions, as the sort of people you are seeking are likely to have a reason other than simple enjoyment for being at the event. They may be speakers with a talk to prepare or stall-holders who need to sell their wares in order to cover the costs of attending. Make sure that you check that they have the time to talk before you ask your questions.

This brings me to another point: try to prepare yourself. Simply asking to be told 'all about Witchcraft' is like asking someone to explain all about the universe in a few words. Try to have a few questions ready and don't forget to ask if you can stay in touch if you feel comfortable with the person you speak to. Of course if you don't feel comfortable, politely move on and try to find someone else.

The advantages of attending events are many, even if you don't find a contact at your first, second or even third attempt. They give you the opportunity to have a look and see what sort of people are around and they provide an excellent opportunity to window shop for books and other items of interest. Generally speaking, they are great fun and are likely to have something of interest for everyone.

USING THE INTERNET

Use of the Internet is increasing rapidly and the majority of people have access, if not through a home computer then through public libraries, Internet cafés and in some cases through school or college, although the latter often place limits on web browsing. The real advantages of the Internet are that you can remain anonymous whilst having a good look around to see what and who is there, you can check out information from all around the world, you can make lots of contacts rather than just one or two close to home and, quite importantly, you can to a limited extent check the accuracy of the information you see before you act upon it. If you browse a number of sites you will find that there are certain 'common truths'. This, together with the information you already have within this book, will give you a basic understanding of what to look for. Anyone who appears to hold views which are greatly different from these is probably walking a different path – not necessarily a 'bad' one, just a different one.

The real drawback to the Internet is that you have absolutely no way of judging people, no real way of telling whether they are truthful and are who they seem to be. However, use of an e-mail address gives you a certain amount of anonymity and whilst you are only communicating through the Internet you can feel secure that no one is going to turn up unannounced on your doorstep!

If, after getting to know someone via e-mail, you feel ready to make further contact, then there are one or two things you should bear in mind. Never give anyone your home address and never give anyone your surname if you have given them your home telephone number. Additionally, do not hand out your work details or those of your school/college. If you observe these guidelines, then you still cannot be easily found. If the person you are in touch with is genuine, they will understand your caution. I don't want to sound as though I see monsters around every corner, but unfortunately you only have to meet one slightly disturbed person or one fanatic who decides they have to convert you to have the whole experience soured.

If you eventually decide that you want to meet your Internet contact, choose a public place, somewhere where there will be lots of people around, and make sure that you can get there and home again through your own resources. Try making your first meeting a casual one, not to discuss the

Craft, just to say hello. Perhaps meet for a coffee in a coffee shop and take a friend who can be trusted not to intrude or who is prepared to sit elsewhere just to observe that everything is OK. Of course you could always arrange to meet your contact at a Pagan event, in which case you have the additional advantage of being able to see others' reactions to them too.

However you choose to make an initial contact, do remember that you have plenty of time. Don't be tempted to rush into things. If it takes two, three or even a dozen meetings before you feel you can trust a person, take that extra time. Once again, if you have any doubts or misgivings, don't be afraid to immediately finish the meeting, and indeed any other communication. Remember that you do not have to meet at all to benefit from communication by e-mail. Many Solitary Witches will continue e-mail correspondence for many years without choosing to meet in person. Indeed, if your correspondent lives on another continent you may never have the opportunity to meet up.

To summarize:

Covens are difficult to locate, especially if you are under 18, and if you are invited to join one whilst still under that age, you should proceed with great caution.

Events require you to summon up a certain amount of nerve in order to approach strangers, even though you are safe in the company of numbers of people, and there will be other things of interest anyway.

The Internet is safe, unless and until you decide to take things further, and it is a great method of communication which can stand on its own.

Whatever approach you take, it is worth taking your time over finding the 'right' person or group of people for you. I know that it is tempting, especially when any kind of contact seems to be in short supply, to take the first offered, but it really is counterproductive to do this. Many are the Witches who have wasted years of their time and energy working with people with whom they feel uncomfortable or who do not have the same view of the Craft as themselves.

When you do find the 'right' person or people for you, you will know it. One of the phrases that keeps recurring in my contacts with those who have found the right group is that 'it feels like coming home'. If you can be sure in your own mind that this is really how you feel and that you are not persuading yourself to feel this way, then you have probably found your niche. This may take many years, but in the meantime you are not wasting your time and energy if you continue to work in the Craft on your own.

ADDRESSES

When getting in touch with these organizations, please always enclose a stamped addressed envelope and remember that some organizations may not grant membership to people under the age of 18 years.

The Pagan Federation

One of the foremost Pagan organizations in the world, whose magazine *Pagan Dawn* provides information on events and contact details for some groups. Members include Witches, Druids, Shamans, those of the Northern Traditions and other Pagan paths.

BM Box 7097, London WC1N 3XX

http://www.paganfed.demon.co.uk [secretary@paganfed.demon.co.uk]

The Children of Artemis

Initiated Witches who seek to find reputable training Covens for genuine seekers.

BM Box Artemis, London WC1N 3XX

http://www.witchcraft.org [contact@witchcraft.org]

ASLaN

Information on the care and preservation of sacred sites all over Britain.

http://www.symbolstone.org/archaeology/aslan

[andy.norfolk@connectfree.co.uk]

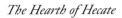

The Hearth of Hecate

The author's group of Covens which also provides an e-mail support service
for Solitary Witches.
http//www.pyewacket.demon.co.uk

The Witches' Voice

One of the best American sources of information about the Craft.
PO Box 4924, Clearwater, Florida 33758–4924
http://www.witchvox.com

Inform

Totally independent and not aligned to any religious organization or group,
this organization's primary aim is to help people through providing them
with accurate, objective and up-to-date information on new religious movements, alternative religions, unfamiliar belief systems and 'cults'.
Houghton Street, London WC2A 2AE
Tel: 020 7955 7654

TERMS AND DEFINITIONS

Some of the words in this glossary have only been touched upon briefly in the text, however they are words which are in common use in the Craft and may well crop up in other books you have read or will read. Other words are also in common usage but have a particular meaning within the Craft and that is the meaning I have given here.

Athame
The Witches' knife or blade. Traditionally a black-handled knife with a double-edged blade nine inches long, the Athame is used when invoking and banishing the elements and other energies. The only thing an Athame should cut is air, or the wedding cake at a Handfasting.

Besom
The traditional broomstick. On one hand this is a symbol of fertility which is literally jumped during a Handfasting to signify the leap from one 'life' to the next. The besom is also used to symbolically sweep the Circle.

Boline	The white-handled knife. This is the working knife of the Witch and is used whenever any cutting, say, of herbs, or carving of symbols is required.
Book of Shadows	A personal record or journal of all your Magical workings, and the thoughts, feelings and results that come from them. Gardnerians refer to 'The Book of Shadows' which was written by Gerald Gardner together with some of his senior Coven members.
Chalice	The Chalice is a symbol of the Goddess and can be made from wood, stone, glass or metal. It can be plain or ornate. What is important is that is contains the wine used in the Rite of Wine and Cakes or in the Great Rite.
Circle	This defines the Sacred Space of the Witch, which is created whenever and wherever it is needed. Casting the Circle is just one part of creating the Sacred Space. A Coven would traditionally cast a Circle nine feet across. However, when working on your own it should be as small or large as your needs.
Coven	A group of three or more Witches (two would be a partnership). Coven size varies considerably, although some consider that a 'proper' Coven should be made up of six men, six women and the High Priestess. The Coven is the family group of the Witches.
Craft	One of the terms for Witchcraft, which has been rightly described as both an Art and a Craft.
Deity	A Goddess or a God. 'Deities' is often used as a generic term for all the Goddesses and Gods, wherever they have come from.

Deosil	Clockwise or Sunwise. When setting up and working in your Sacred Space you should always move Deosil, unless you are undoing something.
Divination	The techniques and ability to discover that which might otherwise remain hidden to us. There are many forms of divination including the tarot, crystal ball, astrology and tea leaves. Witches tend to use the term scrying, although strictly speaking this refers to the Dark Mirror, cauldron, fire or Witches' runes.
Divine	A broader term than deity, the divine encompasses both the Goddess and the God and includes those aspects which do not have a gender or a name.
Elements	The term is often used to refer to the four elements of Earth, Air, Fire and Water, however it is important that the fifth element, that of Spirit, which we ourselves bring to the Circle, is not forgotten. The elements are the keystones of the Craft and refer to aspects of ourselves as well as energies around us. (*See* Chapter 6, 'Magic', for more detail on this.)
Esbat	The Witches' term for Full Moon meetings or workings.
Goddess and God	The female and male aspects of the divine. However, the term 'the Gods' is often used to denote both.
Great Rite	This is the symbolic union of the Goddess and the God. Generally it is performed with the Chalice and Athame. The usual exceptions to this are between working partners and in some forms of initiation.
Handfasting	One of many Rites of Passage, Handfasting is the name for the Witches' wedding. It differs from most 'orthodox' kinds of wedding in that both parties enter

as equals and make their own individual vows to each other. Handfastings can be of different prearranged durations.

High Priestess/
High Priest
The leader of a Coven is usually the High Priestess. She may lead jointly with her High Priest, but holds ultimate authority and responsibility. Some groups are run by the High Priest alone, usually where there is no female of sufficient experience to take this role.

Initiation
Initiation literally means 'to begin'. However, in the Craft initiation is seen as the permanent declaration an individual makes to their Gods. Many of the paths within the Craft refer to three degrees of initiation, each denoting a different level of attainment and ability.

Lore
Knowledge, handed down from generation to generation. Originally oral tradition, a lot of the old lore is now finding its way into books. Much ancient lore which was thought in our scientific age to be superstition is now being proven and accepted.

Magic
The ability to create change by force of will. It is worth remembering that many things we take for granted, like electricity, would have been considered Magic by our ancestors.

Occult
Literally the word means 'hidden'; in medicine 'occult blood' simply means blood that has been found through testing because it cannot be seen with the naked eye. Today the occult is often used as a semi-derogatory term for anything which is not understood and is therefore feared.

Orthodox
A term I have used to identify those beliefs which people tend to think of as older than the supposedly

'New Age' beliefs, when in fact the reverse can be said to be true. For example, people tend to think that Christianity is an older belief system than the modern Pagan beliefs, when in fact the origins of Paganism (including Witchcraft) vastly pre-date it.

Pagan   This is a generic term for a number of pre-Christian religions, Druids, Witches and Heathens to name a few. Pagan probably comes from either the word *paganus*, referring to those who didn't live in the towns – a version of 'country bumpkin' if you like – or the word *pagus*, an administrative unit used by the occupying government. Either way it was originally used as an insult. Now it is a 'label' worn by many with pride.

Pathworking   A Pathworking is a form of guided meditation in which you take a journey that leads to an opportunity to discover more than you already know; sometimes also referred to as 'interactive guided meditation'.

Pentacle   This is a five-pointed star with the points touching but not overlapping a circle. It symbolizes the five elements together with the Circle of power. The Pentacle is worn by many Witches, but is also currently very fashionable, so you cannot be sure whether a wearer is of the Craft or not.

Pentagram   This is a five-pointed star not enclosed in a circle (*see* Pentacle above).

Priest and/or Priestess   In the Craft we are each our own Priest or Priestess, and need no one to speak to our Gods for us.

Quarters   The four cardinal points of the compass – north, south, east and west – which are linked to the directions of the elements.

Reincarnation	To believe in reincarnation is to believe that we return to this world many times as many different individuals.
Rite	A small piece of ritual which, although complete in itself, is not generally performed on its own, such as the Rite of Wine and Cakes. A series of rites put together are a ritual.
Rites of Passage	These rites are specific to marking the change from one stage of life to another, such as birth, marriage and death. Their names in the Craft, Wiccaning, Handfasting and Withdrawal, are different from those in current use, which reflects the different emphasis that Witches place on these events. There are other Rites of Passage but they are less common even in the Craft today.
Ritual	A series of rites put together to achieve a specific result.
Sabbat	A seasonal festival. There are eight Sabbats in the Witches calendar which together are often referred to as 'the Wheel of the Year'. Sabbats are traditionally times of great celebration and festivity. Many of the old Sabbats are still celebrated under more modern names – Yule is known as Christmas, Samhain as Halloween, for example.
Sacred Space	For many religions their place of worship, or religious centre, is a building. Witches create their Sacred Space wherever and whenever they need it, and their Magical workings and some of their celebrations take place within its boundaries.
Scrying	The Witches' term for divination, especially when carried out using a Dark Mirror or the Witches' runes.

Spells and Spellcraft	A spell is a set of actions and/or words designed to bring about a specific Magical intent. Spellcraft is the ability, knowledge and wisdom to know when, as well as how, to perform such actions.
Strong Hand	For a person who is right-handed this will be their right hand, for someone left-handed it is their left. The strong hand is sometimes called the 'giving hand'.
Summerlands	The Witches' name for the place our spirit goes to between incarnations, where we rest and meet those who have gone before us and where we choose the lessons to learn in our next life.
Thurible	Also known as a censer, this is a fireproof container designed to hold burning charcoal and loose incense.
Visualize	This is seeing with the mind's eye so strongly that it appears no different from 'reality'. Visualization is not just about seeing – when you are skilled at it, all your senses will be involved. For example, when visualizing the element of Air you will feel the wind touch your hair and skin, hear its passage through the trees and smell the scents of spring. Visualization is one of the key factors in working the Craft and performing Magic.
Wand	A piece of wood the length of its owner's forearm. In some traditions the Wand is only used where the Athame is not, in others the Wand and Athame can be interchanged.
Wicca and Wiccan	Wicca has been largely adopted as a more 'user friendly' term for Witchcraft. Personally I do not describe myself as a Wiccan, as it simply leads to the question 'What does that mean?' and then you will

sooner or later end up leading to the word 'Witch'. There are some that consider that those who call themselves Wiccans are less traditional than Witches.

Widdershins   Anticlockwise; the opposite to Deosil.

FURTHER READING

There are a great many excellent books on the Craft available today. I have not tried to list them all here but have selected those which I have found helpful to newcomers, whether in a general way or because they specialize in a particular area which is too complex to be covered in an all-round text. If a book is not listed here it does not mean it is not a valuable work, nor is it intended as a slight to the author. Equally, not every book here will suit every reader, as each person has their own requirements in terms of content and preferences when it comes to style. If you find yourself reading something you find tedious or 'heavy going', do not feel that you have a problem; it may simply be that you and that work are not compatible. Some of the books listed have a limited use for the Solitary Witch and I have tried to indicate that in my notes. You may find some of these books are out of print, however it should be possible with perseverance to locate them through the library system. In any case, I would always recommend trying to get hold of a book through a library, at least in the first instance, as in this way you can see whether you like it before deciding to own a copy.

GENERAL BOOKS ON THE CRAFT

J. W. Baker, *The Alex Sanders Lectures*, Magickal Childe, 1984. A perspective on Alexandrian Witchcraft.

Rae Beth, *Hedgewitch*, Phoenix, 1990. Solitary Witchcraft, written as a series of letters to newcomers.

Janice Broch and Veronica MacLer, *Seasonal Dance*, Weiser, 1993. New ideas for the Sabbats.

Vivianne Crowley, *Wicca*, The Aquarian Press, 1989. A general introduction to Wicca.

Janet and Stewart Farrar, *A Witches' Bible* (formerly *The Witches' Way* and *Eight Sabbats for Witches*). Alexandrian Craft as it is practised.

Gerald Gardner, *The Meaning of Witchcraft*, Rider & Co., 1959; reissued by Magickal Childe, 1991. Gardnerian Witchcraft.

Pattalee Glass-Koentop, *Year of Moons, Season of Trees*, Llewellyn, 1991. Information on the Tree calendar and ideas to incorporate at the Full Moons.

Paddy Slade, *Natural Magic*, Hamlyn, n.d. A perspective on Traditional Witchcraft.

Doreen Valiente, *ABC of Witchcraft*, Hale, 1973. Gardnerian Craft written in 'dictionary' form.

Kate West and David Williams, *Born in Albion: The Re-Birth of the Craft*, Pagan Media Ltd, 1996. An introduction to the Craft from the Coven perspective.

SPECIALIST BOOKS ON
ASPECTS OF THE CRAFT

Anne Llewellyn Barstow, *Witchcraze*, HarperCollins. 1995. Detailed history of the persecution of Witches.

Jean Shinola Bolen, *Goddesses in Everywoman*, HarperCollins, 1985. A guide to finding the Goddess within.

Scott Cunningham, *Cunningham's Encyclopaedia of Magical Herbs*, Llewellyn, 1985. Magical uses and tales surrounding most common herbs.

—, *The Complete Book of Oils, Incenses and Brews*, Llewellyn, 1989. Magical preparation and use of oils, incenses and other mixtures.

—, *Cunningham's Encyclopaedia of Crystal, Gem and Metal Magic*, Llewellyn, 1988. Magical properties of most gemstones available today.

Janet and Stewart Farrar, *The Witches' Goddess*, Hale, 1987. Examination of some of the better known Goddesses.

—, *The Witches' God*, Hale, 1989. Examination of some of the better known Gods.

Mrs M. Grieve, *A Modern Herbal*, Jonathan Cape, 1931; reissued Tiger, 1992. A detailed reference for the serious herbalist; identification, preparation and use of herbs, ancient and modern. Also available on the Internet at http://www.botanical.com/botanical/mgmh/mgmh.html.

Barbara Griggs, *The Green Witch*, Vermilion, 1993. A modern healer's handbook rather than a magical reference.

Paul Katzeff, *Moon Madness*, Citadel, 1981. A study of the effects of the Moon and many of the legends and mythology associated with it.

Patricia Monaghan, *The Book of Goddesses and Heroines*, Llewellyn, 1981. A definitive guide to major and minor Goddesses from around the world.

Jeffrey B. Russell, *A History of Witchcraft*, Thames & Hudson, 1983. A factual history of the Craft.

Egerton Sykes, *Who's Who Non-Classical Mythology*. A dictionary of Gods and Goddesses.

Tybol, *Tybol Astrological Almanac*. Annual publication. Diary containing detailed astrological information, Goddess and God festivals, Magical terms and much more.

Kate West, *Pagan Paths*, Pagan Media Ltd, 1997. Six Pathworking cassettes covering the Elements, the Goddess and the God.

—, *Pagan Rites of Passage*, Mandrake Press, 1997. A series of booklets giving information and rituals for Rites of Passage.

Bill Whitcomb, *The Magician's Companion*, Llewellyn, 1993. Possibly the ultimate reference work for correspondences and symbols.